Dec. 2015

Unfinished Chapters

Christina Hamlett, Editor

To Chris and Anna,
Thank you for sharing
your wonderful home with
us, and allowing us to
look after beautiful Luca!
Debbie

DEDICATION

To those who left us much too early.

To those who left without a forwarding address.

And to those with whom we might have shared
a longer conversation.

TABLE OF CONTENTS

ACKNOWLEDGMENTS

With special thanks to the following:

Charlie Plowman, Executive Proofreader

Samya Haddad Mellor, Associate Proofreader

Kyra, JR, Deborah, Kurt and Stacy -
Judges Extraordinaire

And to the authors worldwide who took the time to share their stories

INTRODUCTION
(& the story behind the title)

Not everyone who comes into our lives is destined to stay for the duration. The playmates with whom you were inseparable in second grade. The posse of partying pals you ran with in high school and college. The coworkers who made your office feel like an unscripted sitcom. The neighbors whose kids befriended yours and shared their swimming pool. The close-knit gaggle of confidantes you always called first with good news...or bad.

Yet no matter what assumptions or expectations we hold about the longevity of our relationships, the reality is that they often emerge to fill the needs and wants of a particular moment – a quest for kinship, a salve for loneliness, a pursuit of mirth, a gateway to acceptance, a desire to procreate. Once that moment passes and its inherent lessons learned (for better or worse), it's not uncommon to move on to the next chapter of interesting characters. Yes, obviously some "moments" last longer than others and are a product of genuine symbiosis, respective nurturing, impassioned mentoring, or (on the dark side) codependent enabling.

But what about all the connections that fell through the cracks because of neglect, distance, misunderstandings or simply divergent interests? Such are the address book entries you haven't sent a Christmas card to in years, the alums whose names you only vaguely recognize on the Facebook reunions page, the friends who inexplicably went radio silent and never explained why. Theirs – and yours – are the chapters that forever remain unfinished, leaving one to speculate what might/could/should have been.

The essay competition to find some of these stories yielded an amazing bounty of memories by talented writers across the country and around the world. Some of them shared the pain of losing a spouse, parent or lover to unforeseen tragedy. Others humorously reflected on their first romantic crushes and the flirtations that ensued with strangers they knew they'd never see again. Several dealt with a soldier's call to duty. Many explored the mystifying disconnect between fathers and their offspring.

Choosing the best of the best for publication was no easy task. There is something in each of these essays, however, that will deeply resonate with readers. And if, perchance, you decide to send a copy to someone that has been missing – and missed – from your own life, it will have served its purpose.

And, as promised, here's the story that inspired me to give this book its title.

*****

Los Angeles to Boston is a very long flight. We hadn't even left the tarmac yet and I could already tell it was going to feel even longer. The toddler directly behind me had not only discovered the joys of repeatedly kicking his feet against the back of the seat but also singing the "I love you, you love me" Barney song. On the pretense of getting something out of the overhead, I cast the mother a disapproving look. Her huffy response – easily loud enough to be heard by everyone in the cabin - was that Junior was expressing himself and I should mind my own business.

The situation hadn't gone unnoticed by the flight attendant. As I sat down and re-buckled my seatbelt, she leaned in to whisper that she'd see what she could do. A moment later she returned to tell me there was a seat available in First Class if I'd like to move. She didn't have to ask twice.

The aisle seat was occupied by an attractive woman who reminded me of Natalie Wood. "I thought you'd like the window," she offered. The realization she had switched places for a complete stranger caught me by surprise. My insistence that she didn't have to do that was dismissed with a smile. "I've made this flight more times than I can count," she said. "I'm happy to let someone else enjoy the view." Beneath her breath she added that it also put me that much farther away from the little monster.

"You heard him all the way up here?"

"I'm pretty sure they can even hear him in the terminal…"

By the way she was dressed – a smart navy suit, white blouse and black pumps - I assumed she was going to Boston on business. "Actually I'm going home for a few days," she told me. The trip to Los Angeles had been to attend some meetings and make a speech. "So what's taking you to Beantown?" she asked. "First visit?"

Although I had been there on several previous occasions, the flight to Logan this time around was the pick-up point for a long drive to Vermont. Lyndon Institute's summer program for teens had invited me to teach a week-long class in screenwriting. As I filled her in on my background, she remarked in admiration that it must be fun to be a writer. "Everyone tells me I should write a book," she remarked, punctuating it with a laugh. "You probably hear that a lot, I'm sure."

*****

A part of me felt guilty for being served a First Class entrée that wasn't part of the ticket price I'd paid to travel "steerage." When I commented on it to my companion, she replied that life was too short to eat stale snacks out of a paper sack. "'Bistro' bags are such a misnomer," she quipped. "I can't tell you how many complaints you hear from passengers expecting something Euro." The airlines' recent move to allow passengers to bring their own food on board, she added, wasn't without its own share of problems. "It's like they purposely buy the messiest, gooeyist, smelliest meal they can find and then stuff their leftovers in the seat-back pockets for the crew to clean up."

Since she seemed to be speaking from first-hand experience, I asked, "Are you a flight attendant?"

"Was," she corrected me. "Up until a couple of years ago."

I remembered the wistful envy I'd felt when one of my best friends had gone the "stew" route after graduation and trained for a career with PanAm. While the postcards from exciting places caused me to perceive her job as glamorous, I also realized that the more effortless a flight crew makes the job look, the harder it probably is – a reality my companion was all too happy to confirm as we made our ascent above the clouds.

"If you don't mind my saying so," I remarked, "you seem awfully young to be retired." (Readers may recall that once upon a time there were not only strict age and weight restrictions for flight attendants but also prohibitions against marriage.)

She smiled at the compliment. "Sometimes," she said softly, "the choices are made for us."

*****

As a young woman, her decision to seek employment with American Airlines had been driven in large part by a desire to get as far away as she could from her alcoholic mother. "I loved the idea of travel, of meeting interesting people, of providing the best service possible to make my passengers feel comfortable."

She had also been blessed with a succession of congenial roommates – kindred spirits she nicknamed "the flying sisterhood." The last three of these, she said, had not only been the best but were straight-shooters as well who always believed in speaking their minds and having each other's backs.

A catch crept into her voice as she related the downside of life as a flight attendant. "Although you're meeting new people every day and have the consistency of working with the same crew members, you're basically living out of a suitcase. The furnished apartment we shared wasn't exactly a warm and cozy abode because none of us really had the leisure to go shop for the pretty knick-knacks that would have made it so. And, of course, in the event of a coveted transfer to a different city, who'd have the time or energy to pack and unpack a lot of belongings?"

The social interactions they had outside the context of work often involved the neighborhood bar. "We'd go there to unwind after a long day – even if that day sometimes ended at almost midnight." That they always went as a group meant they made sure none of them drank too much or got into a compromising situation.

"At the beginning, I'd been able to ignore the stress of being on my feet for most of a flight, lifting heavy bags into the overhead, and responding to repeated call-button requests from passengers that wanted to know, 'Are we there yet?'" In addition, there was a commensurate level of depression wondering if she'd ever meet anyone, settle down and have a family. Alcohol not only became the go-to numbing effect she needed to function but also heightened her creativity insofar as disguising its hold on her. "I'd pretend I'd left something down in the hotel bar after we came back to our rooms. I became adept at sleight-of-hand in secretly pilfering mini liquor bottles from the cabin galley. I'd feign a hoarse throat to hide any trace of slur in my voice."

She'd find herself becoming more impatient with passengers, though never to the point of rudeness. "I began forgetting that some of them were genuinely nervous about flying and that their wanting to talk was just to make conversation, not to invade my privacy. There were random acts of niceness and kindness going on all around me but I didn't have time to appreciate or acknowledge it." She recalled one particular red-eye flight. "I liked them because I had the galley to myself and could more easily sneak a bottle into my pocket without anyone seeing me." She was startled when one of her male passengers came into the galley at that very moment to get some water. "It didn't break when it fell but I knew he saw it and, moreover, that he may have suspected what I was doing."

As if to put her at ease, he told her that he was one of those people who couldn't sleep on an airplane. "'Hopefully,' he joked, 'I won't embarrass anyone at my grandson's graduation ceremony if I suddenly start snoring in the middle of it.'" He showed her a picture of his teenaged pride and joy and related that the upcoming celebration was something no one had really expected he would live to attend.

"He looked to me to be the picture of robust health and I wondered whether he had miraculously survived an accident or a life-threatening illness. 'Neither one,' he said, clearly having read my mind. 'I just finally decided to stop denying I had a problem and do something about it.'"

Even then, she confessed, it wasn't a strong enough wake-up call. "No matter how many signs the universe gives you and how many messengers it sends to deliver them, you can always make excuses to ignore them and that's exactly what I did."

A few weeks after that conversation in the galley, she had set her alarm as usual for an early call. Yet despite copious amounts of aspirin and coffee, there was no masking the wicked hangover she had. "My roommates had been coming down hard on me in recent months and trying to police my intake, a move that made me even more defiant … and secretive. I was in no condition to fly. I was potentially putting my passengers and crew members at risk. Although I had yet to be reported – and grounded – they warned me that it was only a matter of time. Their intervention that morning was such that I'd call in sick with the flu, one of them would take my place on the flight, and that I'd agree to check myself into a rehab program when they got back. I remember saying goodbye to them at the front door and promptly heading for the kitchen to make myself a drink."

Her three roommates never made it home on that Tuesday in September of 2001.

"I think of all the people killed that day both in the air and on the ground. So many unfinished chapters that would never be written, so many devastated families that would never again be whole because of a heinous act of terrorism. Time and again I still ask myself why I had been spared when I had made such a complete mess of my life and had so little to live for." Never, though, had she been presumptuous enough to ever speculate that she might have seen something or done something heroic if she had been on her scheduled flight. "I remember the friends who expressed relief I was still alive and all I could think was that I didn't deserve to be."

Because of the last, volatile exchange she'd had with her roommates, she knew she had to honor their memory by getting herself on a strict path to sobriety. "I took a voluntary leave of absence, put myself in the care of a therapist and got into AA. Hardest thing I ever did." She paused a moment before correcting herself. "Actually the hardest thing is knowing I can never take back what I said to three gals who only had my best interests at heart and who couldn't bear seeing what I was doing with the life I'd been given."

It proved to be an epiphany which influenced her interactions from that point on. "You just never know whether that smile you give to a stranger having a rough time is the only thing that might subsequently keep them from acting on suicidal thoughts. Or whether the spare change you give to someone on a corner restores their faith in humanity and inspires them to one day pay it forward. For that matter, we probably won't find out in our own lifetimes the ripple effect of simply chatting it up with a stranger in a slow-moving line, helping an older person get an item off a top shelf at a grocery store, or holding a door for someone struggling with packages, children and a dog."

She smiled. "You never know what sort of chapters they have already lived or what their next chapter will be. What I've come to see, though, is that if their lives or mine were to suddenly end within moments of our paths having crossed, I would find peace in the knowledge that my final curtain was preceded by an unconditional act of kindness."

*****

It wasn't until after we deplaned at Logan, retrieved our luggage and went our separate ways, it occurred to me that we had just traveled the entire length of the country and never asked each other's names. Now and again something will trigger my memory of that flight and I'll find myself wondering how her life has turned out. Did she ever marry? Does she have a family with whom to celebrate holidays? Is she happy ... or at least as happy as she allows herself to be?

Friends with keen analytical minds have opined that it wouldn't be that difficult to find her. While I can't fault their confidence in Google to locate anyone and anything at anytime and anywhere, I believe there are certain connections we are meant to savor only briefly. This was one of them. And though it has joined the ranks of unfinished chapters, such are the stories that provide each of us with a lifelong gift of speculating what their endings might have been.

Christina Hamlett, Editor

GONE THE EXISTENCE OF THEM
By Kelsey Poe
First Place Winner

She walked quietly into my bedroom that morning. The day was progressing, I could tell, because the sun pushed its way brightly through the cracks between the curtains. I sat up in my bed feeling tingly and numb. The tears - hot streaks upon my cheeks - poured out from within me.

"I didn't get to have his babies," I sobbed, doubly hit with the pain of my new reality.

"I know," she soothingly replied, "And he would have made such a good daddy."

She reached for my hand. It was damp and lifeless, and I was embarrassed. Her hands were softened with age, as she must have been in her sixties. They were warm like a grandma's, but I knew she had no grandchildren yet. Her miracle baby was born later in her life, born just before all hope was lost.

She brought me out of the bedroom and helped me get ready. There would be visitors today, mostly my colleagues from graduate school wanting to offer their condolences. They didn't know what it felt like to lose a future just on the brink of it.

A few hours later I was ready, equipped with an emotional wave of strength and social ability. They stormed in like troops (though in actuality, there were only about a dozen of them) bringing discount flowers and dorm food. After they provided me with the obligatory, "I'm so sorry for your loss," they dove into conversations about how the family was coming for commencement in two weeks and the mounting job offers were overwhelming. Then after that came conversations of the much-needed vacations and horrors of house hunting and travails of family planning. I thought I knew them, but suddenly I was cast out.

Then they turned to me, "What are you going to do now?" they asked with morbid curiosity.

Like I have a Plan B?! An in-case-of-emergency card detailing what to do when your husband dies when you're 27 years old?! Are you kidding me?! Get off my furniture, and get out of my house!

"I don't know," I whispered.

The awkward silence hung in the air until there was a knock at the door. In came a gentler soul, well-meaning, though on this occasion, misguided. On her hip was her infant son. The ventricles of my heart forgot how to push fresh blood through, and I thought I was going to die.

"Babies make everything better," she said, turning him towards me.

No, I thought to myself, *not this time.*

I held the baby for an obligatory ten seconds, patted him on the back, and then handed him to the person nearest me. The rest of the room took delight in him, as they did with the rest of their lives, but I sat brooding, mourning, ill-equipped to handle death at such a young age.

Maybe I cast this fate upon myself, I thought. I always chose the harder roads, marrying a man fifteen years older than I was, waiting to have children until the timing was perfect, imagining myself having everything I ever wanted. With my husband's age came wisdom, and he convinced me to wait until after graduation. He was on board with helping me achieve everything I ever wanted and that included college and a career. Then, finally, the time had come where college would be over, and we could begin a new part of our lives. I went to the doctor earlier that month to talk about family planning; I allowed myself to start accepting the dreams of our children as a near-reality.

Then with the death of Sanderson, so also vanished the palpable future. Though I was acutely aware of his absence, I couldn't wrap my mind around the fact that I couldn't have his kids. My mind kept going to the dreams conjured over the years and the plans Sanderson and I made. I kept remembering the wonderful conversations we had about building a family. Those memories were like an escape from this new life of lonesomeness.

I remembered telling him, "You cannot die without first giving me children!" It was always spoken with humor, though the delivery was deadpan because at its center was seriousness. Maybe the deepest part of my soul, the part untapped by human consciousness, knew he would die young. Maybe it's that same part of my soul that continues to believe our children have been real entities waiting to be born.

When he was alive, we would spend Saturday mornings taking our time with the day, lying in bed, and facing each other a nose apart. With speckled kisses and soft caresses, we shared what features we most loved about one another. I always loved his nose; it was cute and unassuming, much like his personality. His black hair was soft and shiny. His eyes were brown, surrounded by a thick layer of lashes. He got them from his mother who was of American Indian decent. We talked softly about what our children would look like and which child would get the best features.

"Our first child will be a girl," I announced, "And she will have my Type-A tenacity and she'll be strong-willed and a leader."

"Oh," Sanderson replied, amused, "How do you know she'll be a girl?"

"Because the world needs strong women," I stated flatly.

"And how do you know she'll be a leader?" Sanderson asked, becoming more convinced of my predictions.

"Well, she has to be. I think in order for her to grow up as a leader, she has to be the oldest child, which has inherent leadership. Besides," I furthered, with an air of knowing-it-all, "If we plan it right, she'll be a Taurus, like me, and we all know how stubborn they are. She'll be strong, and she'll change the world."

Sanderson couldn't argue and probably couldn't help but agree since I had so clearly thought through all the details. To me, these children were not dreams; they were an abstraction about to be revealed in the coming years. They were already real people about to be given life.

The whole family died with Sanderson. We were never going to share the pregnancies and the late night feedings and the grocery store tantrums and the first days of school and that day when we would drop off our child at the college campus, with a farewell to childhood and warm greetings to the seedlings of another generation.

Our children had names; they had faces and personalities. Bianca, our oldest, would prefer to go by "Bibi," except in the boardroom, when she wore a slimming pencil skirt and used presidential gestures. Then, a couple years after Bibi's arrival, Penelope would be born. We'd call her Penny, and she'd grow up to be a news reporter, or something, because anyone with a name like Penny Poe would have to sign off in front of a camera. Then because I never had the twins I always wanted, I would ask Sanderson for the next best thing: Irish twins.

"Honey," he'd cajole, "You just had Penny; it will be so hard to chase after her with a newborn. You'd have two kids under the age of one. That's a lot of diapers."

"But you're so close to your brother, and you were born just less than a year after him. I want our kids to have siblings as best friends. I want that bond for them." I'd open my eyes a little brighter and demurely tilt my chin down. He'd sigh in resignation because he knew there was no talking me out of things. He trusted me.

So, just before my body would give out, I'd have Jasper. "That boy will be the death me," I'd say, but secretly affirming his every ADHD action. He'd have the spirit just like his father – an adventurer, a risk taker, where his curiosity would lead his actions. He'd be bright and witty and grossly independent.

Then one day, later in his life, he'd meet a young woman at a coffee shop. She'd stop him cold in his tracks because, to him, no other woman existed like her in the world. She'd be the compass he needed, guiding him, supporting him, sometimes tilting her chin down to persuade him. And for her, he would set her free from all her self-inflicted burdens. He would caress her skin and tell her that she could do anything in this world, and she'd believe him and then go do it. His voice would resonate in her soul, and so Jasper would become not just the greatest gift to his mother, but to his wife as well.

Then that fateful day would arrive, when his soul would depart the earth. The heavy hearts of those left behind would sink in broken sorrow. All the dreams dreamt up in bed on Saturday mornings would vanish because their realities were contingent on life. All the people in heaven, waiting to be born on Earth, would put their hands on their chest, right where their beating hearts would have laid. They would shake their heads as they look at each other. Then they would turn around to go back from where they came. The singular echo of one man's laughter would resonate, his joy would appreciate in value, but his dreams would be lost.

****

Kelsey Poe is a writer and counselor. She lost her husband in 2013 and has painstakingly found a way to move forward in life, carrying with her the sweet memories from a man who supported her unconditionally. She is currently residing in Paris, France, with the promise to follow her dreams.
www.kelseypoe.com
@kelseylynpoe

DEAR "BONEHEAD,"
By Catherine S. Blair
Second Place Winner

I never understood why you took such pleasure in our shared nickname. You could have chosen to call me *Dictionary* or *Goober Glasses*, like the rest of our third grade class, but you were never one to conform to the rest of the crowd.

Do you remember how we met? A head-on freeze-tag casualty during morning recess. Mrs. M told us that she was surprised we still had brains in those heads of ours after the collision, but we didn't even feel dizzy. "You're a bonehead!" You yelled at me, angry that we never made it back to the safe zone to evade capture.

"No I'm not, you're a bonehead!" I glared right back at you, and doubled my fists. Instead of fighting, you laughed, and just like that a friendship was born.

In fourth grade you were constantly cutting in front of me in the lunch line and tugging my pigtails. There was no reason to shoot spit bombs into my hair, you know. If you had just asked me, I would have told you that I thought you were cute and I liked to watch you beat the rest of our class at tetherball and four square.

In fifth grade I wore bright red coke-bottle glasses that obscured half my face, a mouth full of metal, high-waisted uniform skirts and knee socks. Did I mention that I was the facilitator of an unofficial class newspaper? Can you say, "Nerd alert?" Fifth grade was the year I received a new nickname, *The Computer*, but that didn't stop you from yelling "Hey, Bonehead," at me across the room. "What's up, Bonehead?" I would shout back, laughing as Mrs. B turned around to glare at us.

I'll never forget the time you let the class chinchilla loose and all the girls jumped up onto their desks screaming hysterically. I think I laughed so hard that I cried. You tried to look repentant when you were held back from recess for a week without snack, but I'll never forget the look on your face when I stole a handful of soda crackers and passed them to you in a napkin that I stashed in my jacket when Mrs. B wasn't looking. My heart was beating so fast that I was sure you would hear it when I pretended to bump into you so I could drop the crackers into your lap. You ignored my sweaty palms and thready pulse and grinned up at me. "Thanks, Bonehead." That whisper was enough to make my cheeks flush red for the rest of the day. I was old enough then to realize that guys who looked like you were not supposed to be nice to girls that looked like me.

When sixth grade rolled around you and I were sorted back into the same classroom. On the first day of school we waited for our assigned seats, and guess whose desk was right next to mine? This was a great year. We spent most of our free time drawing stick-figure cartoons and playing tic-tac-toe in our desks where Mrs. K couldn't see us. I think that was the year that I fell I love with you, the last of the wonder years.

See, Bonehead, I never told you how I thought you were the coolest, funniest, most awesome guy in our grade. I never tried to hint that I wanted you to ask me on a date, like all those other not-so-subtle girls in our class. I never had the courage to kiss you back, that one time that we promised never to speak of again (writing it down doesn't count), when you ambushed me in the bushes at our end of the year picnic.

I tried to forget your voice in my ear when you whispered, "I love you, Bonehead," but I can still hear the words clearly. I stared at you, dumbfounded, as you smashed your lips against mine and then grinned, before running off. Things were different between us after that.

In seventh grade you joined the football team, and I joined the jazz band and the art club. We didn't have any of the same classes, mainly because I was only carrying honors credits and you had to retake basic math. Once, we passed each other in the hallway and you were surrounded by a group of big, rowdy, football players. I met your eyes and looked away before I could see a look of disgust on your face, but when you passed by me I heard you say, "What's up, Bonehead?" It was as though we were third graders again, whispering in the classroom together and building rubber cement glue balls.

If life were truly a fairytale, this would be the moment when I, the ugly duckling, grew into a swan, declared my love for you and you swept me into your arms and we lived happily ever after. Unfortunately for me, we both grew up and went our separate ways. Before long we made it to high school, and you were made a starting quarterback while I won the election for vice president of the student council.

Did you ever hear me cheering for you at those football games? I should have gathered my courage and gone down to the field to congratulate you when you guys went to States.

Instead, I chose to love you from afar, and I don't think you ever knew. How could you have?

Graduation has long since come and gone. The last time I saw you was when all of our classmates gathered on the field after project grad; we stood in a big circle on the lawn and hugged all 350 members of our senior class. When I stopped in front of you I could feel my heart filled to brimming with all the words I wanted to say, but all I could manage was a strangled, "Goodbye, Bonehead," and that was more like a whisper anyway.

I have come a long way from that shy, nerdy girl who stuttered when she got nervous, liked to recite poems in Pig Latin, and thought it was cool to quote *Oliver Twist* during any and all occasions. I wouldn't say that I am now a bona fide swan, but I did manage to lose the braces, buy some contacts, grow a few inches, and learn how to use the gym equipment and walk in a straight line without tripping over my feet.

I've been on a few dates, and I'm currently seeing a guy who calls me "Kitten," or "Sweetheart," but never "Bonehead." He's smart, funny, and recently graduated from law school, but when I asked him if he used to sniff Mr. Sketch markers or tie peoples shoelaces together under their desks, he looked at me like I had grown a third head.

And then I received your letter.

Did I ever tell you that my dad is a pastor? I highly doubt my monosyllabic responses ever equated to that knowledge, but he is. My dad is the guy your fiancée called to officiate at your wedding next summer. I've thought about you a lot through the years, always wondering where you ended up and what might have been if I had more courage. Now, as I stand here holding this wedding invitation and staring down at your smiling face, I can finally put you to rest.

Bonehead, in this photo you are laughing wildly, as you and your almost-bride hang upside down in a tree, holding a handmade sign that says, "Save the date, we're getting hitched!"

I look at you and I see the eight-year-old class clown who stole my heart along with my lunch money. Congratulations on finally finding a woman who is brave enough to finish your duet.

I don't know if it's too late for me to cultivate a little more bravery in my life, but here goes. I asked my dad to give you this letter the next time he sees you. It might not mean that much to you, but I want you to know that your friendship meant a lot to me. You might have always been the funny jock, loved by the masses, but this nerdy, over-achieving, goody-goody was far from a swan. I've always wished for the opportunity to tell you what you meant to me back in the wonder years, and now here goes. My friend, thank you for seeing me, in all of my broken-down, imperfect glory and teaching me what it felt like to be loved.

Here's to wishing you an exceptionally happy marriage, and a future filled with laughter, life, and a whole lotta love. I hope that fiancée of yours knows that she's got a keeper!

Yours truly, The Original "Bonehead."

****

A historian by trade and a writer by choice, Catherine S. Blair grew up gorging herself on "Once Upon a Time's." She cut her milk teeth on garage-sale paperbacks and satiated her hunger for words by re-writing her own happy endings. In addition to continuing a successful career in academia, Kanani is currently working on preparing her debut novel for publication. She believes that one good story has the power to change the world.

LOVE ME DO
By Tracy Falenwolfe
Third Place Winner

I've heard the story many times. The year was 1964, and the Beatles were coming to play at the 4-H Club in my tiny hometown. The crowd gathered. Girls swooned. And then the house lights went down and the band took the stage. Except instead of John, Paul, George and Ringo in the spotlight, the band members were my father and three of his friends donning Beatles wigs and toting cardboard instruments. They called themselves The Four Shadows, and from what I understand they really delivered; their performances were a regular thing and well-attended. But the band had to break up when the shadows got drafted.

I didn't know this about my father when I was a child. When I was growing up, my family wasn't particularly open. We slogged through one day after the other and didn't talk much about the past. We didn't talk much about anything, least of all how we felt about each other. My parents did call each other "Hon", but it never dawned on me that it was short for honey. I'd always heard it like Hun. As in Attila.

My father was much stingier with his emotions than anyone else in the family, so much so that I couldn't imagine how we'd even *become* a family. Fueled by a combination of curiosity and insecurity, I was always searching for clues that would solve the puzzle of my very existence.

When none appeared, I concocted excuses for my father: Maybe it was Vietnam that made him so apathetic. Maybe I reminded him of someone else. Maybe I wasn't really his. I felt like he resented me for simply existing. For being in the way somehow. He was always coming home from one job and going right off to another, and I wondered if it was just a way for him to get away from me.

I could never find any hard evidence supporting any of my theories regarding our lack of a connection, and believe me, I looked. I poured over family photo albums that chronicled my life with a repetition that should have made any child, even me, feel secure. Birthdays, holidays, vacations, nothing had escaped the lens. It was all there, year after year, in black and white in the beginning, and then in brilliant Kodachrome.

But there was always space between my father and me in those pictures. I couldn't find a single photo where he'd put his arm around my shoulders, or held my hand, or kissed my cheek, or even sat close. I couldn't remember if the gap between us had been there since birth, or if it was forged by some later disappointment, yet indelibly etched in my mind was his irritated expression whenever my feet grew and I needed new shoes - as if the twenty he had to fork over for a pair of The Winners from Sears was the one he'd been saving for a bus ticket to his new life in Reno, and I'd just ruined his plans.

Eventually I married and had my own kids. By then, I'd seen those pictures of my father in the Beatles wig. There was a light in his eyes and a smile on his face in those shots that had faded after I came along, and I wanted to know where it went. I was like Richard Dreyfus's character in *Close Encounters of the Third Kind*: distracted, obsessed, crafting mountains out of my mashed potatoes, knowing that I possessed some knowledge, some truth about my father that I couldn't access, and wondering what it all meant.

Meanwhile, my father doted on his grandchildren, favoring the youngest, whoever that was at the time. When the family was all together, he'd take all the kids downstairs to the playroom and feed them candy and teach them to shoot rubber bands, or cap guns, or whatever else my husband and I and my brother and his wife didn't let our children do.

Once, when my oldest son was two, my father gave him a Lifesaver. He almost choked to death, but my father was unfazed. "He wasn't supposed to swallow it," was all he had to say. The "dumb kid" was implied. But later, I overheard my son say "I love you, Pop-Pop," and my father responded, "I love you, too."

I'd never heard those words come out of his mouth. He'd never said them to me, or to my brother, or to my mother, as far as I knew, yet over the next several years I'd hear him say it to each of his grandchildren at least once. It gave me hope, but I was still afraid to ask, "Do you love me, too? Did you ever?"

I'd wanted to know, wanted to hear it for thirty-some years, but at this point I didn't want to ruin anything for my kids. Maybe my father only had so much love to give, and he'd only just discovered it or had somehow saved it for his grandchildren.

Either way, he'd changed. I'd changed too. My kids teased me when I balked over the price of a winter coat for one of them. I wasn't irritated. I wasn't saving for a bus ticket. But I'd hoped, for that amount of money, anyway, that I could get more for my kids. That I could *give* them more.

And maybe I started understanding why my father had always seemed so disenchanted when I was growing up.

That Christmas, my brother and I gathered the five grandchildren to sit for a portrait. I had to buy a frame for it, but I didn't want to take the kids to the store with me, so I called my parents to babysit. I was apprehensive when I heard my father was home alone. It had been seven years, but after the Lifesaver incident, no one left the kids with only him.

I did it anyway. When I got back, I found my offspring in the playroom sweaty and covered with rubber band welts. Their faces were smeared with chocolate and peanut butter. "How much candy did you give them?" I demanded, taking in the pile of red, green, and gold spent wrappers on the table. My father shrugged like he had nothing to do with it. My kids complained. "You're back already?"

One of them held a pair of drumsticks. The other had a fake guitar slung over his shoulder. They'd been playing Rock Band with their grandfather, and I had interrupted. Call me Yoko.

I ushered the kids up the stairs, and then for some reason I looked back at my father. He seemed tired, but he smiled. The look on his face was one I'd never seen. He said nothing, but he didn't look away. It was as if he were taking a snapshot of me in his mind. Like he wanted to remember that particular moment, which didn't seem special to me at all.

Later, as I wrapped the portrait in its frame, I arrived at the conclusion that things were as good as they were ever going to get between my father and me. Whether he loved me or not, he loved my children, and that would have to be enough.

My father never saw that family portrait. He died of a sudden heart attack two days after I bought the frame for it. He was fifty-nine years old. There were no warning signs, but when I remember the look we shared two days prior to his death, I think he knew it was coming.

He'd been shoveling snow when it happened. Sometimes I look at the spot on the sidewalk where he fell. I no longer see his lifeless body there staring up at the heavy gray clouds. I see the scorch marks from him setting off fireworks every summer for my enjoyment. I see the above- ground pool he put up and maintained for me to swim in, yet never had the time to enjoy himself. I see the empty spot where there used to be a post next to the walkway—the one he took down because I kept running into it on my bike.

I remember him working two jobs – always - and then in his "free" time installing the purple shag carpeting I'd picked out for my bedroom when I was twelve. Knocking on my door with a birthday present he'd purchased for my mother and wanted me to hide somewhere. Putting toys together on Christmas morning - probably his only day off from both jobs that week or month or year.

I see him building a snowman with my kids. Hiding eggs at Easter. Slipping me money to buy snow boots for my boys. (Before their toes pressed up against the fronts of the old ones.)

My father never said the words. He never held my hand, or put his arm around me. He never called me his little girl or told me everything was going to be all right. In my mind's eye, he'll always be wearing a tool belt and walking away from me. And still I am sure he loved me. I am sure, because in all the years I waited for my father to say the words, I never said them to him, either.

I hope he favored me when I was the youngest, like he did with his grandchildren. I hope I giggled when he played with me. If he played with me. Sometimes I wish I could animate a photo I found of him holding me at my christening. I long to see the moments just before and after the shutter closed. I hope he kissed my bald head and smiled. I hope he bounced me up and down a bit before handing me off to someone else. But it's okay if he didn't. Every single thing he did in the thirty-six years after that picture was snapped shows that he cared.

I hope he was happy, but it wasn't really in his nature to say if he was or wasn't. I wish there had been time for a Four Shadows reunion tour; that my father hadn't worked up until the day he died; that I had gotten to see firsthand the sparkle in his eyes, the grin on his face, when he'd been a carefree teenager up on that stage with no worries and no responsibilities, strumming a cardboard guitar and singing at the top of his lungs.

But most of all, I wish we hadn't been so alike. I wish that one of us had broken down and said the words. Because now that it is too late, I look through the old photo albums and when I see the space between us I realize he saw it too. I've gone from wondering if he loved me to wondering if he knew I loved him, and it's agonizing. On a good day, I view those unspoken words between us as the legacy he left me and his grandchildren.

My boys are teenagers now. I don't want them to ever have to wonder if they are loved. I hug them even when they try to get away. I kiss them even when they wipe it off. I say the words a lot. I would love them even if they didn't love me back. But since they were old enough to speak, the sweetest music to my ears has always been hearing the words my father never did: "I love you, too."

****

Tracy Falenwolfe lives in Northeastern Pennsylvania with her husband and two sons. Her work is featured in the forthcoming anthology A Readable Feast, published by The Bethlehem Writers Group, LLC. She is a member of Romance Writers of America, Mystery Writers of America, and Sisters in Crime.

SECRET LOVE
By Terri Elders

"You're 15, right, babe? So you can catch grunion without a fishing license?"

After all these years I still remember how I whirled around from my open locker, my ponytail nearly smacking Eddie McDaniels' chin. His sea-green eyes searched my face, as if he'd find my birthdate inscribed right there on my forehead or cheeks. "Right?" he asked again.

"Yes, I'm 15. So?"

He flashed me a crooked grin. I closed the locker door. "Julie's waiting for me," I said, edging down the hall towards the exit.

Eddie fell in beside me. "Uhh," he began, "Would you come with me to the Dude's beach party at Tin Can Beach this Saturday? It's a grunion run. We'll roast hot dogs and marshmallows."

I stopped and peered up at him. Was he asking me out on a date? Those ocean eyes, that sun-bleached flattop…I could nearly smell the salt air.

I hoped he wouldn't notice how I'd turned tomato red. Every time I heard Doris Day sing *Secret Love* on the radio, I daydreamed that Eddie would turn out to be more than just my neighbor. We lived on the same block, but in radically separate worlds. I was a "socialite"; he was a surfer. Nonetheless, we had a kind of arrangement. I helped with his homework; he protected me from neighborhood bullies. I idolized him. I kept it a secret, though. You wouldn't catch me shouting about my love from the highest hill or telling any golden daffodils. I was nowhere near as brave as Doris Day.

Once one of our English teachers questioned whether Eddie really had written the report he turned in on Steinbeck's The Pearl. She called him a lounge lizard and glowered at me. I met her gaze without flinching, but after school I hurried to a dictionary. Lounge lizards sponged off women. I wanted to tell Miss Schmidt that Eddie was no sponger. Because it involved the sea, he had loved that book. He wrote his paper straight from his heart. I just edited it a bit.

My friends had another disparaging name for Eddie: beach bum. While Eddie didn't particularly shine at school, he positively shimmered at the shore. He didn't fall into any other category. He wasn't a motorcycle outlaw, a hood or a Beatnik; he simply surfed. In my eyes he was a surfer king.

"Well?" Eddie asked, shifting from foot to foot in a kind of rangy lopsided shuffle.

"It's a real run, right? No snipe hunts or submarine races?"

Eddie laughed. "Word. The grunion will make the scene. If you're under 16, you don't need a license. The rangers show up, we'll say the batch belongs to you, that you caught them all. It'll be cool."

I stared up at him as I thought it through. Tin Can Beach had a dubious reputation. It derived its name from rusted cans whose lids menaced the bare feet of unwary sunbathers. Nonetheless, vacationing families could pitch a tent, build a bonfire, and camp out there for free. I'd heard that during the Depression people down on their luck even lived there all summer.

I'd never visited the place, just had driven by with my family on the way to visit the Fun Zone at Balboa. My "socialite" friends, the kids who made honor roll, played in the band, produced the school paper, favored Hermosa Beach, where all summer we'd slather ourselves with cocoa butter, body surf and parade up and down the boardwalk sipping Orange Julius shakes. A year earlier two of my girlfriends had tried to teach me to smoke in the women's bathroom. That was about as daring as anybody got at Hermosa.

In those mid-50s days the serious surfers would hang ten at San Onofre or Malibu. Tin Can Beach drew a different crowd...the guys who swilled beer, siphoned gas, and made out with girls at the passion pit drive-ins. Guys like the Dudes. And like Eddie. Eddie didn't talk much about the Dudes or surfing when we did homework together, but I'd heard the rumors. He was considered a bit rough, a bit rowdy.

But a grunion run! Since childhood I'd read of this uniquely Southern California phenomenon, the slippery sardine-like silversides that swarmed ashore at high tide to lay their eggs and spawn. Few of my crowd had seen a run; fewer still had been agile enough to capture any of the tiny fish. Even if I were there only as a lookout for rangers, I'd still be with Eddie. And I'd have been to a grunion run, a landmark event.

"All right, Eddie. Just promise... no beer. My dad would have kittens!"

"Crazy, babe. Later!" Eddie sprinted back up the corridor and I exited towards the quad. I could hardly wait to tell Julie.

"Eddie McDaniels? You're loco," Julie said, rolling her eyes, just as I knew she would.

"Hey," I countered, "If we actually catch any grunion, I'll have a topic for my science report!"

Julie shook her head. "Just be careful," she cautioned, "The Dudes are pretty wild."

"I trust Eddie," I said, remembering how he'd stood up for me years before when the kids who'd congregated on our corner had thrown spitballs at me when I'd roller-skated by.

That Saturday I dressed carefully in jeans, a pink pullover sweater and saddle shoes. I took extra care tying back my ponytail with a pink grosgrain ribbon, and applied a little mascara and Pink Queen lipstick. I even splashed some Aphrodesia cologne behind my ears and on my wrists.

Despite the balmy spring air, I knew that even summer nights could turn chilly at the beach. I borrowed Dad's black leather jacket, promising to take good care of it.

"You look pretty cool, babe," Eddie said when he picked me up. I ducked my head so he wouldn't see me blush. The last thing I wanted him to know was how much his casual compliment meant to me.

By sundown the Dudes had a bonfire snapping and crackling. I threaded a pair of wieners on a straightened out wire coat hanger and started to roast them. Eddie declined an offer of a beer, and fished a couple of bottles of Coke out of an ice-filled washtub.

"Hey, Eddie, what's up with the Coke? Is your date a wet blanket?" A couple of the Dudes frowned in my direction. I held my breath. I didn't want to hear Eddie denying that I was his date or explaining that he'd only dragged me along to act as a decoy.

Eddie ignored them though, and just walked over and handed me a Coke. "Hey, babe," he whispered, "Don't get frosted at those guys. Sometimes they go ape at the beach. They don't know no better." He sat down beside me on an old Army blanket he'd taken from the trunk of his old Chevy. My hot dog tasted pretty good, even without the mustard, which I'd skipped to avoid dripping anything on Dad's jacket.

Under the radiant full moon it was easy to pick out the couples now cocooned in their blankets. From time to time I could hear a pop as another beer can lid was skewered by the punchers the guys called church keys. But Eddie and I just sat quietly, eating our hot dogs and gazing out at the sea, waiting to greet the fish. We had our flashlights and gunny sacks ready.

Soon we heard a shout from down the beach, and then the shoreline lit up as everybody rushed forward, waving flashlights. We bolted for the water. As the fish-filled waves broke, Eddie dug at the sand, snatching up handfuls of grunion while I held open the bag.

Suddenly one of the Dudes drew near. "Hey, Eddie," he yelled, "Gonna be a killjoy all night long?" He waved a beer can around wildly, flicking foam towards us. I backed away, terrified of staining Dad's jacket.

Eddie stood his ground, motioning me back towards the fire. I watched him wait for the next wave, then tackle the menacing Dude just before it broke. He laughed as froth from the overturned beer mated with froth from the waves.

"Come on, babe," he said. "Let's cut out. I'll take you home. You don't have to lie to the rangers for those jerks. Good thing no beer got on that jacket!"

When we got to my house, Eddie offered to walk me to the door, but I declined. I wanted to avoid any awkward goodnights on my porch. I didn't want Eddie to think he was obligated to give me a hug...or even more embarrassing, a kiss.

"It's OK. The porch light is on, and my folks are still up." I hopped out of the Chevy and started up the walk.

I saw Julie on Monday morning. "Well?"

"The Dudes were wild, but Eddie protected me. He always has. So I guess I'll help him write his science paper on the grunion, instead of writing my own about them." Julie just laughed.

I didn't see much of Eddie that summer and when school started he didn't show up. I learned from his brother that he had gone to live in Hawaii with some cousins. He'd finish his senior year in Honolulu. Years later on a cable television show I saw him again. He was as bronzed, sun-bleached, and ocean-eyed as ever and he'd just won a surfing trophy. Still chasing a wave.

Not long ago at a high school reunion I ran into that menacing Dude from the grunion run. "Yeah, I remember you. You were the wet blanket that time when that big Kahuna, Eddie McDaniels, dunked me in the surf," he said.

"That was me," I agreed. "But, man," I continued, "the wet blanket I remember most was the one you wrapped yourself up in after you took that unexpected tumble into the surf."
I smirked, just as if I were fifteen again.

Secret loves aren't secret if anybody ever knows. I'd never told a soul about my love for Eddie, not even Julie. A few minutes after I'd bantered with the Dude, Eddie McDaniels walked into the party. Though his hair had turned completely silver, he still looked tan and fit. I held my breath as he approached me.

He just stood there, staring at me. Finally he nodded. "Babe," he said, "When we were kids you had a crush on me and I knew it. I was going to tell you how much I cared for you the night I took you to the grunion run. I was going to ask you if you'd wait for me until we both grew up a little. But

I was a chicken when you jumped out of my car. I should have run after you. I've always regretted that I didn't."

Once again I turned tomato-red. This time I didn't duck my head. But I stifled a sob as Eddie McDaniels after five decades finally took me in his arms and kissed me. It was worth waiting for. He held me tight until my husband walked up and asked to be introduced.

I winked at my husband. He winked back. He understood about love and kisses…and memories.

****

Terri Elders' first byline appeared in 1946 on a piece about how bats saved her family's home from fire, published on the children's page of the Portland Oregonian. Aged nine, she hadn't known that her title, "Bats in Our Belfry," would lead readers to suspect her family's sanity. Unrepentant, she continues to spill the beans, sharing secrets in anthology stories. Her indiscretions have been featured in more than 100 books, including such series as Chicken Soup for the Soul, A Cup of Comfort, Thin Threads, and HCI Ultimate. She's a "co-creator" for the Not Your Mother's Book series. http://atouchoftarragon.blogspot.com/

ONE REGRET
By Josephine Harwood

My mother was beautiful, extremely modest, and very classy. She was intelligent and her laughter was contagious. She encouraged and supported me, and she was always there whenever I needed a shoulder to cry on. She was my hero. The only thing missing on her was a cape. She was practically immortal and indestructible.

And when she finally passed, I was angry with her for leaving me.

Twice.

She had suffered a ruptured brain aneurysm causing a massive stroke stealing the memory of those who loved her. My husband, my rock, loved my mother very much. He insisted my parents live with us so we could help them. To say the caregiving experience was overwhelming would be an understatement. I had recently given birth to my first child, and I had no previous caregiver training. Needless to say, diaper changes took on a whole new meaning for me.

There wasn't much of an outreach program for family caregivers in the late 80's. Whenever my father would become frustrated or overly stressed, I would remind him that his wife didn't come with instructions.

While my father was on the golf course taking advantage of his much-deserved daily break, I would play my mother's favorite music or turn on the television when it was time for one of her favorite shows. Depending on her level of alertness, she would communicate with me using few words. I could gain her attention by singing to her, and sometimes she would remember the words and sing along with me. She was very sweet and smiled most of the time, but she treated me like a kind stranger. Recognizing me or verbally acknowledging me as her daughter would rarely happen, and those moments were like a precious gift beyond price.

My mother and son developed a loving bond. Sometimes, we would place the baby in her arms, so she could hold him or feed him with the bottle. As my son grew, we would help her to the floor so she could play with him. He liked to walk around her wheelchair and try to climb up on her lap, and she would lean forward to receive his hug. Although she had left-side neglect, and she was supposed to be incapable of turning her head to the left, she moved her head easily as she followed my son as he moved around the room.

My mother would also respond very well to my husband. Before her stroke she told me she liked following him in a buffet line, because he always found what she liked to call, *the good stuff*. After her stroke, she had little or no appetite and protein shakes replaced her daily meals. Sometimes my husband could fix a plate of food, and she would want exactly what he was having. He could easily encourage her to eat.

Although she recognized my father even less often than me, I had discovered something intriguing. One time she was unusually alert while I was feeding her, and I had noticed her following my dad with her eyes as he walked across the room.

"Mom, do you know that guy?" I asked.

She shook her head slowly and asked, "Who is he?"

Casually I replied, "Ask him."

Looking directly at her husband, Earl, and without any hesitation she said, "Earl, what's your name?"

I have never forgotten this moment, because I had thought her responses meant she was trying to come back to us. Every morning I would wake up filled with anxiety and hope that today would be a better day than yesterday. Today, she would recognize us a little more often than before. Today, she would be a little more independent. She would continue to get better.

Living in denial was so damned easy.

As the years went by, she continued to deteriorate both mentally and physically. She was practically bed-ridden with a stomach tube, but I was blind to her declining condition. I insisted on taking care of her, and I adamantly refused outside help. No one was going to touch my mother. No one was going to feed her or change her diapers.

No one was going to put her in a nursing home.

When her body began to fold up, knees to chest, I was unable to straighten her legs. Changing her diapers and clothes became more challenging, but still I insisted I could handle it. I knew in my heart as soon as my mother was admitted to a nursing home she would never forgive me for abandoning her, and she would give up and die.

I also arrogantly believed if I gave her enough love and enough care, I could stop her from dying this way.

My mother's doctor insisted we place her in a nursing home. I was deeply offended at first but then she pointed out something to me that I hadn't realized before. She told me for the past four years, my husband has always had his job and my father had his daily golf games. She wanted to know where I went when it was my turn to have a break from my mother.

I broke down and cried because I didn't have an answer for her.

When I shared this with my father and my husband, they cried with me and told me it was time to place my mother in a nursing home. I was the reason she was still at home. They had been waiting for me to admit there was nothing more we could do for her.

We finally placed my mother in a nursing home.

She died four months later.

I remember thinking that chapter in my life was closed, and it should be fairly easy for me to get over the loss and move on. When my father started drinking heavily, I turned to a grief counselor for help. I promised to go with my father if he would agree to meet the counselor. I never dreamed I would end up in counseling, too. I had a lot of anger inside of me that needed to be addressed and resolved. I hated my mother for dying on me, twice, and I hated myself for not doing a better job taking care of her.

Through therapy I learned that forgiveness is the greatest gift that people can give to themselves.

In the past 26 years, I have been a family caregiver for my mother, my father, my father-in-law, and currently my mother-in-law. I jokingly tell people I don't remember signing up for this, but I strongly believe you never know what you can do until you have to do it.

Caring for a loved one can be mentally as well as physically exhausting. It can feel like a wall that has fallen against your back and continues to weigh you down. You are determined to keep the wall from falling, but asking for help means admitting defeat. Admitting defeat is not an option.

You can handle this.

But when the wall becomes heavier, there is a part of you who wishes secretly there was someone to help you, to give you a break … even if it's only for one precious hour.

Stop feeling guilty. You have more than earned this right.

You are not abandoning your loved one. You are recharging, remembering how to breathe, again, and reminding yourself that your loved one did not come with instructions...and you are doing the very best you can.

Family caregivers are superheroes, but remember all superheroes have a weakness.

Here are some possible signs of your Kryptonite.

You experience mood swings, your immune system is shot, you are easily irritated, you have no energy to exercise, and you have no social life.

Remember to put away the cape every now and then, and ask for help!! Let someone rescue...YOU!!

So, what is the one regret I have for taking care of my mother?

I wish I had spent more time enjoying my mother and less time worrying about everything else.

****

Josephine Harwood has been a family caregiver on and off for more than 26 years, and she is passionate about reaching out to other fellow caregivers on her Facebook page, Empathy & Caregivers 911. She enjoys listening to classic rock music and reading romance novels. She treasures quality time with family and friends, and she cherishes the unconditional love of her three rescue dogs. She is easily inspired by her husband of more than 30 years to write romance novels. She has self-published two books, "Dark Secrets" and "Empathy," and she is currently working on a sequel for "Dark Secrets".

STRANGERS ON A MIDNIGHT BUS
By Charlotte Nystrom

Many of us encounter hundreds of people every day. Yet, we don't stop or speak. We continue along our paths, remaining strangers. It's as if there are these invisible boundaries with an illusion of safety inside. Sometimes temptation gets the best of us, though. We tiptoe over the border, toying with social norms.

This is the sin which I committed that late December night. One minute we were two strangers blending into the crowd. I was the country girl heading home from college for the winter break. I exited the sleepy Greyhound into a frenzy of action. Colored lights flashed and swirled on a multitude of screens. There were people everywhere. The Port Authority Bus Terminal exploded with bodies frantically moving this way and that. I knew I had only fifteen minutes until my next departure. I struggled to read the signs without getting swept into the current. A security guard appeared out of thin air and motioned his hand towards my ticket, which I readily obliged. He led me in the right direction. I nearly had to run to keep up. Having reached the assigned location, the uniformed man wished me a good night and disappeared.

That's when I saw Andre for the first time. He was standing there near the gate, looking exceptionally relaxed. He smiled in my general direction. I clutched my ticket and lowered my backpack, giving my shoulder a moment of reprieve. I smiled back hesitantly. He removed his headphones and sauntered over. I noticed the comfortable sag of his lounge pants and matching hoodie. I found myself in a moment of jealousy, handicapped by blistered heels, tight jeans, and a constricting fitted jacket. I wasn't prepared for socializing, but that didn't discourage him.

"I just have to run outside real quick. Can you watch my bag for a minute?" he asked, nodding towards an over-sized duffle.

"Sure thing," I responded and immediately regretted. It was the sort of thing easily accepted in my natural habitat, but I was far outside my element. I'd seen too many late night specials. I imagined that the bag was filled with explosives and a ticking timer that was about to go off. Or worse, it held a substantial amount of cocaine or blood diamonds. Maybe the guy was under surveillance and I was about to take the fall. It was too late for a change of heart, he had already vanished into the fray. I sweated it out until he returned.

"Thanks," he said.

"Yeah. No problem," I replied with a sign of relief.

"I'm Andre, by the way."

"Oh, It's nice to meet you Andre…I'm Charlotte." I stammered.

"How are you doing today?" He asked sincerely.

"I'm good thanks. And you?"

"Are you really? Or are you just being courteous?" He stared into my soul, forcing me question my automated response. Was I good?

"No, I'm really good. No complaints here. Life is great," I assured this stranger.

An announcement was made and the line we had been standing in started to lurch forward. I handed my pass to a female boarding agent. She punched my ticket while offering a knowing glance. I wondered what she knew.

I climbed the steep stairs onto the bus. Andre was ahead of me. He sat near the back and motioned for me to join him. Feeling shy, I chose a seat near the middle of the bus. Two nearby teenagers giggled from across the aisle.

"That guy wants you to sit with him in the back. Do you know him?" One asked.

I shook my head.

They rolled their eyes and returned to their attention to their handheld devices. Andre grabbed his bag and parked himself beside me.

"Dude, if she wanted to sit with you she would have gone back there." The other teenager piped up defensively.

"It's all right," I assure him, wanting to avoid a scene.

"Are you sure?" Andre asks. "I can move."

"It's fine. Sit where you please."

The engine rumbles and the lights dim. It is nine o'clock. We will be dumped off in Boston around midnight. The other passengers quiet down and get comfortable.

Andre leans close and whispers. He wants to know everything about me. He asks about my family and where I am headed, where I go to school, what I am studying and why I'm so beautiful. Ignoring the last question, I do my best to answer the rest before turning the tables. He is going to Alabama to stay with an aunt and work in construction. I suggest he might be headed in the wrong direction. This bus is headed north.

The four-hour trip from upstate had been long and lonely. It was nice to have a companion for this leg of the journey. Still, there was a smidge of discomfort that wouldn't allow me to fall sleep as I had intended. Two hours into the conversation, he pulled that lame routine. He faked a stretch, only to let his arm land lazily around my shoulders. I laughed softly and grabbed his hand, kindly returning it to his lap. He brazenly entwined his fingers with mine. I let him. We continued toying with each other through conversation. There was chemistry.

We talked about everything and nothing. I was struck by his animation and the way his dimples collected the moonlight. He wasn't particularly tall, but he was certainly dark and handsome. In moments of awkward silence, I watched the skyline as the bus sped along its intended route. There blur of city lights was hypnotizing.

The attraction was still pulsating from our pores when the bus pulled into the next station. No one moved when the driver opened the door. A violent commotion spilled into the parking lot. A woman was yelling and threatening to smack someone. I held my breath. Eventually, she ran off in hot pursuit of her prey. We filed into the terminal. I moved slowly. I had a six hour wait until the final bus would arrive to take me home to Maine.

Andre and I stumbled over to a bench and sat down. His connection would be leaving in just a few minutes.

"Well, it was nice knowing you. Have a safe trip." I said.

He gave me a quick hug and walked away. I thought that was the end of our encounter. I found a bathroom and freshened up, then got a large coffee from one of the vendors. A creature of habit, I prepared my return to the same empty bench.

It wasn't empty. Andre was there in all his glory. I wasn't alone just yet.

"Well, hello again." I smiled, genuinely pleased.

"I got a new ticket. There is another connection that leaves in four hours. That's four hours more that I get to spend with you."

I was blown away by the devotion of this stranger. It was clear that the muddled emotions were mutual.

Having had enough of sitting, we decided to take a walk. First, we explored the concourse and all of its culinary delights. Andre insisted we have our first date. He treated me to a stale raisin bagel loaded with cream cheese. It was the first food I had eaten in more than twelve hours, yet I couldn't muster much of an appetite. My stomach squirmed with butterflies. I took a few nibbles to be polite.

After our one-star dinner, he talked me into venturing outside. Fresh air sounded marvelous, but he was still a stranger beckoning me out into a strange city. I caved.

We took a walk through the desolate streets, dancing more than anything. It was freezing and thrilling. The nauseating scent of his cigarette clung in the air. There was no shortage of sidewalks to assault or windows in which to peer. The snow began to fall heavier, it was becoming impossible to see. We retreated back into the safety of the suffocating station. This time we sat on a wooden bench near the entrance opposite a blaring work of art. It was a silent but loud exhibit, overflowing with brilliant colors. It existed in stark contrast to the blank and open spaces of the concourse.

We sat there, still chatting away, as if there were no limit to the things we had to say to each other. I had just broken up with a boyfriend the week before. He willed me to expand on everything that had gone tragically wrong. It wasn't the end of the world. I was in college. The world was just beginning.

Andre stretched out on the bench, resting his head in my lap. I caressed his hairline as he told me about his brother and the roofing business he hoped to own someday. We had fallen into a dreamy and intimate space, suspended between our real lives and everyone in them. Suddenly, we became painfully aware that we were not alone.

"You should be doing that for her," a voice shouted. It was a custodian. He was an older man with a crooked back, carrying a dustpan and broom. "You should be making your wife comfortable, not the other way around, my boy."

"No, I'm not his ... I mean we are only ..." How could I tell this old-fashioned fellow, who seemed to believe in chivalry and kind manners that we two intimate beings were but strangers in the night?

The custodian left and Andre kissed me. He kissed me hard and passionately, as though he had years of pent-up affection to share. What shocked me most was the inhibition with which I kissed him back. We spend the next hour as lovers about to come undone. We kissed and touched. We pulled each other close. Nothing else existed, until it did; the time was drawing near.

"I could stay with you, until your bus comes." He offered.

"But then you will miss your bus again. No, I can't let you do that. You are already late. Your aunt will be worried." I insisted. There was no point in delaying the inevitable. We didn't fit in each other's lives. This night would soon end and all the magic would die with it.

"At least give me your number so I can call you tomorrow. Please, I've never known anyone like you," He begged.

That was the moment that a future me would question. I agreed in words, but not in heart. I did the thing that any 19-year-old female would do. I made up a series of digits that weren't mine. We were parts of different worlds that could never collide beyond that station. How could I explain his existence to my mother or roommate if he called?

He dictated his number for me to transcribe inside my journal of poetry and prose. I didn't quite catch the last two digits, nor did I ask him to repeat. I had no intention of calling.

His bus arrived and pried us apart. A small piece of me is stuck there in that station. That bittersweet moment sits unresolved. What might have been if I had been a braver sort of girl? Did Andre make it to his destination? Were any of his words the truth? Perhaps our children would sit quietly and listen to an edited version of the day when we met. Maybe we would have grown cold and distant until we could no longer stand to breathe the other's breath. If we crossed paths today in a crowded place, would he recognize my face?

Ten years later, my memory refuses to shake the smile of a handsome stranger. If I close my eyes, I can remember the smell of his cologne and the warmth of his touch. Our encounter could have changed everything, but in the end it changed nothing.

****

Charlotte Louise Nystrom is a creative writer and poet from the rocky coast of Maine. She spends her time giggling with her treasured son or wandering the fields and forests in search of inspiration. Her pen flows freely each night when the rest of the world is safe in slumber. She is constantly haunted by characters that beg to be brought to life. Her work is honest, emotional and raw. More than anything, Charlotte strives to capture the words that will touch her reader's hearts and souls.

AN UNFORGETTABLE COMBAT MOMENT
By Robert B. Robeson

Combat is a unique setting for issues of the heart, because the stakes are so high while attempting to survive moment by moment in a brutal world that encompasses the most lethal competition known to humanity. There's already a massive built-in level of stress. It's life or death. It's simply human drama, danger and destruction at its zenith.

As an American soldier serving during the war in Viet-Nam, I was aware a person couldn't always do as he wished in life. Yet often you did what you must. I also quickly learned that not every act of heroism in combat is marked by a monument. Many exist only in the remembrances of those who were there. That's why even today, more than 45 years later, one special infantry medic's courage is still fresh, compelling, painful and inspiring. Vivid memories of him continually return like "phantom pains" felt in limbs long ago lost. As William Makepeace Thackeray so aptly stated, "Bravery never goes out of fashion."

In January 1970, I was a U.S. Army Medical Service Corps pilot and operations officer assigned to the 236th Medical Detachment (Helicopter Ambulance) located at Red Beach on the edge of picturesque Da Nang Harbor. I'd assigned myself to a week of standby duty with three other "Dust Off" medevac crew members at our field site, battalion aid station at Landing Zone Hawk Hill, 32 miles south of Da Nang along Highway 1.

My flight medic had become a close friend with a medic who was assigned to an infantry company co-located with us there. About midway through that week, my medic mentioned his friend wanted to meet me because he'd heard I was a published writer. Writing happened to be one of his main goals and interests, too.

Heavy enemy action was present in our 5,000 square mile operational area during this time but one hot and hectic afternoon, between a host of medevac missions, my medic was able to arrange a meeting in our aid station which overlooked surrounding rice paddies and bunkers silhouetted against rows of concertina wire encircling the entire base. I remember I'd been told this infantry medic was 19 years old. Physically, he wasn't someone you'd expect to be on the offensive line of the NFL's Denver Broncos. He was short and slender, but God had put more into him than anyone could tell from the outside.

We stood out of the steady flow of traffic near the entrance, next to our radio shack, while wounded patients were carried in on bloody stretchers from another medevac helicopter out of Chu Lai--a unit farther south of Hawk Hill--that was unloading on the landing pad outside. We quietly talked about writing and flying for twenty or so minutes before another mission was called in and my crew had to scramble. But during our brief conversation, this teenager barely out of high school, whose name I can't recall after all these years, looked squarely into my eyes for a long moment and then softly spoke words I haven't forgotten.

"Sir, when you get back to 'the World,' tell them what it's like here. Tell them what we're trying to do."

"I will," I replied quickly. We shook hands again before I hurried outside to fire-up our Lycoming
jet-powered bird.

I remembered my momentary interaction with this intense medic, who had brown hair and eyes, when the numbing news reached me more than a week later in operations at our unit headquarters in Da Nang. His platoon had been out on patrol when they were ambushed by a larger enemy force. Their point man had been seriously wounded and became separated from the rest when their platoon leader ordered them to fall back and regroup while he called in an artillery strike on the enemy position. The point man could be heard calling for medical help above the ensuing firefight.

Everyone was aware that in this type of guerrilla warfare North Vietnamese Army troops would often not kill a wounded American because they knew he would lure comrades back into the kill zone in an attempt to save him. They knew how highly we prized life. Although enemy fire continued unabated, and he was warned not to approach the point man until the artillery strike was over and reinforcements were en route, this motivated medic began removing his web gear.

"My job is to get to him," he said to those nearby. "I'm going. He shouldn't have to die alone."

After setting down his gear and weapon, and only taking his aid bag, he crouched and crawled about 50 meters back through the confusion and enemy fire to his wounded buddy trapped between the opposing forces. That's where he was later found lying next to his friend. Both were dead, having been executed at close range, even though neither of them had a weapon at that time. They escaped the "surly bonds of earth" together somewhere in the Que Son Valley southwest of Da Nang in I Corps. Only God knows what happened between them in their final moments in this life.

I believe he knew he was going to die that afternoon because of what he'd said to me in the aid station. Perhaps it was a premonition of injury or death stated by so many other soldiers I met there that ultimately came true. He wanted to be a writer, too, but yet he asked *me* to "tell them what we're trying to do." His commitment to a fellow American, though, held a higher priority. That's probably why he left his weapon behind and any opportunity to defend himself or his patient. He didn't want it falling into enemy hands, too. He chose not to cast his lot with the survivors because a seriously wounded comrade facing a lonely and painful death needed him more. For this reason, his light in our world was quickly extinguished.

There had been nothing tough or fierce-looking about this young soldier. His small stature and supposed noncombatant status hardly matched the more traditional gung-ho "grunt" type. But, in retrospect, his eyes had expressed a lot more than what could be seen on the exterior, because they were windows into a very special soul. They had an intensity and depth of feeling in them that was almost palpable.

He was awarded a posthumous Silver Star, America's third highest medal for heroism, but he'd given us so much more in a war where there were no welcome homes, no parades, no brass bands, no grand speeches, no bunting and no yellow ribbons "tied 'round the old oak tree." He lived a short violent life and was buried somewhere in the land he loved and served so faithfully with little fanfare.

When I safely returned, after flying 987 medevac missions for more than 2,500 patients from both sides of the action during that traumatic year in Southeast Asia, I made a commitment to myself to do everything in my power to inform others of what we had experienced there. I wanted to remember and highlight the actions of those who attempted to provide freedom to those who had none of their own and honor the thousands of Americans who would now never be able to experience a long life of freedom themselves.

I also promised myself to tell everyone possible about this courageous infantry teenager who knowingly sacrificed his life so a buddy wouldn't have to die alone. In the Bible, Jesus said it best in John 15:13 (KJV): "Greater love hath no man than this, that a man lay down his life for his friends."

The experiences and feelings of military personnel who've been in combat, and the significance of those events on their lives today, are not always easy to talk about or for those who've never been there to understand. Combat is noisy, exhausting, brutal, bloody, often terrifying and incredibly uncomfortable. Officer and enlisted personnel, alike, grow to totally depend on each other in order to survive. Since then, nearly five decades have flowed beneath the bridge of my life. But now a day seldom passes--either in the silent darkness of night or the first glow of morning--when I don't reflect on or recall events from my generation's war or the 20-minute conversation with that infantry medic. Sometimes these experiences and that infantry medic's unforgettable words seep into my brain, drop by drop. Drips and drops collect and, before I realize what's happening, suddenly there's a puddle I have to deal with.

After many futile efforts at tracking down my flight medic who'd introduced us that day, failed attempts to discover the name of the infantry medic by his approximate date of death through various military organizations, and painstakingly combing through my notes and old letters written while in Viet-Nam, I decided a visit to the Vietnam Veterans Memorial was past due.

A few months prior to retiring from active duty, after more than 27 years of military service on three continents, I flew to Washington, DC. It was time to say goodbye to some gallant and special friends whose names share equal billing on this magnificent memorial. "The Wall" also notes the brevity of human life in time of war. Any war.

If I couldn't remember or discover this medic's name after all those years, at least I knew he was symbolically buried in the order they were snatched from us and would be listed near the beginning of the panel marked "1970." It would be prior to fellow medevac pilot and friend Capt. Jack B. Hallstead's name on line 58 of panel 11 west, who died in a helicopter crash on April 27, 1970, between Da Nang and Phu Bai.

I made three trips to the Wall during that visit, once in the middle of the night, and felt the closest I've ever felt to him since that January afternoon in the aid station at LZ Hawk Hill. *Some of us are made to live on this earth for a long time and others for a short time,* was a thought that continually coursed through my mind as I stood silently before that black, V-shaped granite presence. Having been raised in the home of a minister, I've always believed that God is the only one who knows why it's this way.

Memories of unflinching head-on heroism in combat die slowly for those who have witnessed it and I now know that courage can only be measured by its own yardstick. It's not calculated by size, sex, social status or race, but rather by deed.

For me, this dedicated soldier's voice still echoes down the long hallway of my mind. Although I can't recall his name these many decades later, I can still visualize him standing next to me in that aid station's dim light as though it were yesterday. Sometimes all a person can do is hold what is left of such an experience until the pain subsides or one's own life slowly slips away.

There's an old saying, "Don't let a man be known for the last thing he does. Let him be known for the best thing he does." But sometimes, as in this medic's case, the best thing *is* the last thing.

Today time ticks remorsefully on. Yet whenever I think back to all the brave young men and women I was privileged to know and interact with in combat, he heads the list. He did all he
Could ... and more. Now he belongs to eternity - one complete cycle beyond our earth-borne vision. I'm fortunate to have had an opportunity to meet him, if only briefly, and will always remember this supreme sacrifice made by a unique and special American soldier who will never again be with us in this life. His warm and wonderful memory is a spouse which tolerates no divorce. Such companionship becomes a part of one's soul and cannot be obliterated. In the end, I thank God for giving him to America, if only for a short 19 years.

****

Robert Robeson is a retired U.S. Army lieutenant colonel who served for more than 27 years on three continents. He flew 987 helicopter medical evacuation missions in Vietnam (1969-1970), had seven aircraft shot up by enemy fire and was shot down twice in one year while evacuating more than 2,500 patients. He has a BA in English from the University of Maryland-College Park and has completed extensive undergraduate and graduate work in journalism at the University of Nebraska, Lincoln. He's also been a newspaper managing editor and has been published more than 850 times in 300 publications in 130 countries.

THOSE WERE THE DAYS, MY FRIEND
By Debbie McClure

When I was in public school, I was devastated to learn that my teacher was having me repeat Grade 7. My friends that I'd gone through school with up to that point would go on and I was humiliated to learn that I wouldn't. I agonized all summer about how to deal with the shame and tragedy. I thought I was pretty smart, so how had this happened? Well, for one, I knew my nemesis was math. English was my favorite subject, and one at which I excelled. Math, not so much. I couldn't believe that I was going to have to repeat an entire grade, and year, just because of one stupid subject! What I didn't know then was that life has a way of teaching us lessons we need to learn, whether we want to learn them or not.

The September of the year I returned to Grade 7, I hung my head in shame. I hated feeling "less than" everyone else. Many of the friends I'd chummed with the year before didn't want to be seen with me. Failing a grade had me doubting myself in every way possible. Then I met Kathy. I'd seen her around plenty of times, and because we lived in a small, close-knit subdivision, our mothers knew each other via various home and school programs. As the bell rang to announce recess one day, Kathy approached and asked me if I'd like to hang out. She was younger than I was by a full year, but she looked friendly and behind her glasses, her eyes shone with bright laughter. Shrugging my shoulders, I agreed. That was the beginning.

For the next four years we were inseparable. We walked to and from school together, we hung out, we talked about boys, we got into trouble together, we met other girls to hang out with, and we had a blast. I remember hot summer days at the beach, and long walks just "hanging." We talked about anything and everything. Nothing was sacred.

When Kathy's parents separated, she was devastated, so we grew even closer. Oh sure, there were other girls we were friends with, but really it was the two of us, always. Her home and family were almost as familiar to me as my own, and there was a feeling of belonging between us. When we started high school, we were both so eager to join the ranks of the kids who'd gone on before us. We were playing in the big leagues now. We took up smoking, and thought we were pretty cool. It was all good.

Then we started meeting and dating boys. We double dated a lot and talked endlessly in our bedrooms about the boys. We experimented with make-up, and giggled about sex. We didn't know it then, but we were still children playing at being grown-ups. We thought we knew it all and had it all together. The music of the seventies, like Elton John, Pink Floyd, Simon and Garfunkel, Paul McCartney's Wings, and countless others echoed our sentiments of life and we reveled in our freedom and youth. There was nothing we couldn't do or be. We shared dreams of what we'd do when we grew up, and agonized over romances that fell flat. Secret dreams and aspirations, along with outrageous laughter, were the glue that held us together.

When I told her I thought I'd like to be a writer, she didn't laugh and make me feel ridiculous. Instead, she encouraged me and said it would be great if I could someday be a famous author. What fun!

Looking back, I can still clearly remember, like a photograph or old video, lying on our backs in the afternoon one perfect summer's day. We were maybe thirteen or fourteen, and we were describing the clouds to each other. At one point Kathy looked over at me and said, "We're gonna be friends until we're really, really old, right?" (Note: "old" probably meant around thirty or forty years of age.) I nodded and reassured her we would. Nothing could come between us. I hardly ever thought about being held back a grade anymore, and had regained my confidence in so many ways I could never have envisioned.

Little did I know that I'd dishonor that vow in just a few years. It started when Kathy introduced me to the boy who would later become my husband (and ex-husband). At first we were all friends and double dated many times, but eventually I realized that Kathy and my boyfriend didn't really care for each other. Kathy claimed he was too "bossy" and she just didn't like him. My back went up in defense of my new love, and we quarreled. I was hurt that she didn't like this boy I was starting to fall in love with, and slowly but surely, the times we all spent together started getting fewer and fewer. I told myself I owed my loyalty to my boyfriend, and that she was just jealous, but deep down, I knew I was wrong.

On my wedding day, I remember getting ready to leave the house with my father for the short drive to the church. I stepped outside in my beautiful white gown and even though I couldn't see Kathy's house from mine, I looked down the street. We hadn't spoken in months, and my heart was heavy that she wasn't going to be there to watch me take the biggest step of my life. I'd heard from her older sister that she was away for the weekend with friends, but I kept hoping against hope that she'd materialize around the corner and we'd get over our petty differences. I was missing my best friend, but wouldn't admit it to anyone. I squared my shoulders, telling myself she had deserted me and that I didn't need her friendship. I was a grown woman now, and was about to embark on a new life, leaving my childhood behind me. I thought I had all the answers.

Shortly after I married and moved away from home, I heard that Kathy moved out west to Calgary. We never saw each other again, and many, many times over the years I've wondered how she is. I've seen her mother a handful of times over the years, and each time I ask how Kathy is doing. Of course she's married now, with children and grandchildren of her own. Life went on for us both, and we moved on. After thirteen years of marriage, I divorced my husband, realizing in hindsight that Kathy was right; he wasn't a wonderful guy who just needed me to understand him.

Following my marriage, I spent a lot of years as a single mother living on the poverty line, then finally happily re-married, and now have a slew of fabulous children and grandchildren. Despite all the ups and downs I've experienced in my life, I feel pretty fortunate for the people I now call family and friends. At age fifty I became the writer Kathy encouraged me to be, although not quite famous. Those old dreams never died, but they did go dormant for many years while I sorted out the business of living and raising my children. Along the way I've learned a lot about who I am, and who I want to be, but every so often I think of those days when I had a best girlfriend who knew me inside and out and had my back.

A few weeks ago I came across a song I used to love, *Those Were The Days*, by Mary Hopkin. As I sat and listened to the words, I was transported back across time to a much simpler past. I could clearly see Kathy's laughing face and hear her calling my name. I can never recover those days, and Kathy still lives in Calgary, so it's unlikely we'll see each other again. As I said, life teaches us lessons, whether we want to learn them or not. I walked away from a friend and have regretted it for almost forty years now. I've had many friends in my life over the years, some of whom still remain, and others who passed through, and new ones I treasure. Kathy saw what I couldn't, and I refused to listen. Maybe this was a lesson I had to learn the hard way, as with so many others I've learned. I wish I could say I'm sorry for turning my back on our friendship, but in my heart I'll always thank her for befriending a sad little girl and making her feel good about herself again. After all, it is the greatest gift one person can give another.

****

Following a 10-year career in real estate and mortgage sales, Debbie A. McClure is the author of "In The Spirit Of Love"/Echelon Press 2012 and "In The Spirit Of

Forgiveness"/Echelon Press 2014. She now writes full time from her home near the quiet lakeside village of Grand Bend, Ontario, Canada with her husband. In addition to her writing, Debbie enjoys connecting with others via public speaking events, writing workshops, regular blog posts, social media, and her books. For more information on Debbie and her work, please check out her website at www.damcclure.net.

THREE WORDS
By Clifford Protzman

It may not be the most popular three-word combination, but to me they are the most powerful. I could feel my facial muscles form a smile, as I stared into my daughter's eyes. She was moving to a new job 1,500 miles away. She was scared and excited. We had passed into the second phase of the parent-child relationship. She was now a young adult, out of school and on her own. I no longer had a teenager. It was no longer my job to take care of her. Supporting her choices was now my mission.

She simply said, "Thank you, Dad." Hearing the words brought me such warmth and happiness. I regretted never saying them to my father.

My father was a tall, soft-spoken man. He was never a strict disciplinarian, unless prodded by my mother. Dad would most likely talk about why I shouldn't misbehave rather than punish. As I became a teenager our talks became more complicated.

Dad had played semi-pro ball. My first Christmas present was a ball and glove from my father. From the first moment I gripped a ball, I began a lifelong love affair with the game. My father understood my love of the game, yet never pushed me to be the star he wasn't. We always had baseball.

In my youth, after my Little League games, we would sit on the front porch. The discussion would center on the day's game, good plays and bad. Our talks were his way of being involved and connected. He had the talent of making a point with a subtle comment. On many occasions we discussed other subjects. The normal pressures of growing up infected the simplicity of our relationship. However we always came back to baseball.

The year I turned 15, it appeared that I might have a future in baseball. My father continued to talk baseball, but he was adamant that I prepare for a future outside the game. Our conflict exploded after a game that summer.

Dad pulled the car into the garage as we arrived home after that game. My mother and brothers headed into the house. As I got out of the car,

47

Dad grabbed my bat bag, slinging it aside and simultaneously grabbing my arm with his other hand. "Let's take a walk." He led me around the house to the back yard.

As we cleared the corner of the house he turned to face me. "Were you trying to make an ass of yourself?" I was stunned.

That game will not be remembered by any of the participants except for me. My team was undefeated and playing a weaker opponent. The score mounted steadily to a 20-0 lead at the end of six innings. Following a time honored tradition, my teammates didn't mention that I had a no-hitter. I knew it. Walking to the dugout after the sixth, I needed just three more outs to finish it. Coach met me at the steps. I was expecting words of encouragement. Instead he said, "I'm taking you out. We need you later this week." The league rule was if a pitcher pitched more than six innings in a game he couldn't pitch again that week. We had two more games that week and he wanted me available.

I was furious. I screamed at Coach, "I want to finish this. I deserve sole credit for this." My teammates joined in. Voices were loud enough to be heard throughout the park. Finally he relented. I went to the mound for the final inning. I was still steaming. Third pitch of the inning the batter ripped a double down the left field line. I was now in a rage. I started blindly throwing as fast I could. Pitches were flying from my hand like lightning strikes with no target. When the inning was over I had given up several hits, hit two batters, and allowed three runs.

Dad was still standing in front of me, staring hard into my eyes. I was afraid to say anything, not knowing what was coming next. He started, "You're a teenager acting like a two-year-old throwing a temper tantrum. You lost control out there."

It was my turn to be mad. "But Dad, I was pissed off. It was my game. Coach was going to take it away from me." The words were already out before I realized my mistake.

"The minute you lost control of yourself, the game was no longer yours. Your behavior embarrassed your team, your coaches and yourself. You're not a child. You want to play with the best? It's time to grow up."

It was dark outside. The stars and the lights from inside the house provided the only illumination. We were quiet now. He was allowing me to think. I slowly realized we were not talking about a baseball game.

He put his arm around my shoulders steering me toward the back door. I said, "I wanted it. What would you have done?"

"Well, you have a hero. They teach us to be better. Next time, think how would Roberto Clemente handle it."

That night didn't resolve all the conflicts between father and son. Destiny intervened five months later.

It was New Year's Day 1973 and I had been up late the night before watching the festivities on TV. Who was knocking at my bedroom door at this hour of the morning? The sun was barely up. It had to be my mother. Although she usually ran the vacuum outside the door if she thought I should be awake early on a day off. It couldn't be my younger brothers knocking; they knew better.

I had turned 16 last week. I believed I was now old enough to decide my wake up time, on a holiday no less. I rolled over to look at the clock radio and the time was 7:45. AM!! The knock came again, and I heard my father call my name. I rose and leaned on my elbows in bed.

"Come in."

The door cracked and my father leaned his head in. He was not angry, but had a look I could not interpret. I knew immediately something was wrong.

"You may want to get up and listen to the news. It's..." I heard his throat catch. "It's Clemente... His plane is missing."

My head, still groggy from sleep, became number if that was possible. It was the name. Everyone in Pittsburgh and the baseball world, my world, recognized the name. In Latin America the name Roberto Clemente was revered.

I pulled the covers off and stumbled to the radio to tune in KDKA. The announcer was saying that the search continues and there are no sign of survivors. His plane was taking relief supplies to earthquake victims in Nicaragua when it went down. Relief efforts in Nicaragua had been hampered by local corruption and Clemente wanted to ensure the supplies reached those in need.

I turned and told my dad, "I'll be up in a minute." My mind was still groggy, but not from sleep.

I slowly looked around my room. There were the two World Championship pennants from 1960 and 1971; Clemente was named MVP in '71. Hanging next to the pennants was the newspaper picture of him standing on second base, tipping his helmet to the world after collecting his 3,000th hit, his eyes glowing as he acknowledged the crowd. That was just three months ago, his final at bat of the season. Only 10 players in the previous 96 years had accomplished that feat. His eyes glowing as he acknowledged the crowd.

I shuffled from my room through the family room and up the oval staircase to the kitchen. My father was sipping from his perpetual cup of coffee. My brothers were already up, drinking orange juice and eating cereal. The radio was on with ongoing news of the Clemente story. I poured a bowl of Wheaties and joined them.

The conversation began. What happened? What are they doing? Will they find him? It seemed like a bad Lifetime movie and shortly we would hear there was a miraculous rescue. The day continued like that. We ignored the college football bowl games and listened to news reports from the radio. There was no CNN in those days.

My dad was never a Clemente fan. He often tried to convince me that the players of his generation were better. It was an ongoing lively debate between us. And yet there were tears in his eyes as he said to me, "Heroes never die."

The news announcer reported that rescue was unlikely. The search had been called off for the night. No wreckage or survivors had been recovered. As the days passed there was no closure. The story continued, but his body was never found.

The Baseball Hall of Fame elected Clemente immediately. His credentials were without question. An MVP award, four batting titles, a .317 lifetime batting average were only a few of his accomplishments. It was his concern for underprivileged people that made Clemente bigger than just a ballplayer. Major League Baseball named its humanitarian award after him.

I had never truly felt the loss of someone in my life until that New Year's Day. There would be no more games for Clemente to play. The emptiness and heartache would replace the excitement of watching him take the field. His regal manner of competition was gone. Clemente would never again stride slowly to the plate with confidence and composure.

The Pirates scheduled a memorial ceremony honoring Clemente on opening day the next season. That was also the opening day for my high school team. That opening day for me was eerie. I trotted to my shortstop position, but somehow there was a greater urgency then winning a game. It seemed like this game meant more to my life than just the final score. Was baseball just a game or a future? I was no longer a kid playing a game.

My father passed away five years later from a heart attack. I didn't realize it then, but I had again lost a hero. I was barely out of college ready to begin a career. I was no longer playing baseball. I did coach the game when my daughters were old enough to play. I followed my dad's lesson. I used the game to start conversations with my teenage daughters.

In every life there is an event that defines change. New Year's Day 1973 was that moment for me. The world I lived in had changed. Baseball was still important to me. However, there was a future to plan outside the diamond. Who was I going to be? The choices and options were formidable and overwhelming. In hindsight, the chosen paths proved to be a mixture of positive and negative.

However, in life, as in baseball, there is always another game to play. Like a series of baseball games, my life was a victory one day, a loss the next day, just hoping to hit a winning streak.

Life's memories fade from our thoughts as time passes. I will always remember that backyard talk with my father. When facing difficult situations, I reach for the composure my father taught me so long ago. Heroes teach us to strive for the better.

I regret never saying, "Thank you Dad." I hope he took comfort knowing Heroes never die.

****

Cliff Protzman had a 30-year career in the world of finance after attending the University of Pittsburgh. He is currently working on a mystery series located in his hometown of Pittsburgh, Pa. The series focuses on the underbelly of the financial world. Cliff has been published in the Pittsburgh Post-Gazette commenting on his beloved Pittsburgh Pirates. In December 2014, he was invited to read his short story "Prime Suspect" for a Celebration of Short Fiction at Barnes & Noble in Boardman, OH.

HIT AND RUN
By Chaynna Campbell

"No one forgets his or her first" - especially if they left tread marks proving how fast they sped off. A hit-and-run leaves you with immediate shock, pending questions, and alone to repair the damage. How you deal with it will determine the next few stops of your journey to recovery.

Blissfully unaware of the oncoming trouble, I saw no reason for caution. I found myself lucky to be with him. He was incredibly hardworking, sweet and considerate which is why the hit came out of nowhere. I began to idolize him and that was my first mistake. The sudden hit threw me completely off course. In a foggy mess, the headlights of my own naivety blinded me. Late one night, a good friend called me and asked if Lucas and I were still dating. I giggled, "As far as I know, why?" She grew hesitant, but eventually summoned the words; "'Cause his ex just posted intimate photos online of them at Six Flags."

My heart dropped to my stomach and my knees dropped to the floor. I desperately hoped his ex was just recirculating old pictures. Feeling as if someone sucker-punched me in the gut, I gasped for air. I took a deep breath and begged for her to be mistaken, ruling out if they were old pictures or not. She confirmed the photos were recent and they were definitely an item again. Bringing all my questions to a screeching halt, he ignored any form of contact I attempted, including phone calls, texts, e-mails, and dodging our mutual inquiring friends. But he was lost in his own world with her. We lived towns apart and I knew getting a ride to his place was completely out of the question. I can't even say it was because I still had a bit of dignity left; it was because I couldn't find a ride. I can chuckle at this now, but back then I was at my lowest point, seeking answers as to why all of this happened.

My devastated mind couldn't fathom it and I went into a deep, depressive state. I couldn't keep anything down besides bread and apple juice. Food lost its taste, all colors appeared dull, and I was too tired to do anything, yet I couldn't get more than two hours of sleep a night. The sleep deprivation stage didn't last more than a week; after that I started crashing hard. Everything else, though, continued for months.

I, of course, obsessed over every petty thing I could've done differently. Maybe I wasn't pretty enough. Did I wait too long? Why her? (The usual compulsive, insecure tendencies following a failed relationship.) Then I stopped. I stopped thinking *what if I bump into him in the future*, what I'll say, how I'll react. It was pointlessly time-consuming and it prevented me from moving forward. I couldn't stay stuck in one spot forever. I bitterly assured myself I'll take the high road and just keep cruising. That was the plan, set in stone, sealed with a lock, and tied with a bow ... until he e-mailed me. *Now* he wanted to talk and now I'd finally get the answers I desperately needed, but didn't want to hear. I was at a crossroads contemplating if I should give him a chance to redeem himself.

He wanted to meet in person if I agreed. Apparently things turned sour between him and his ex-girlfriend and he wanted us back together. I read the message over a dozen times. I gave him the green light and agreed to talk, but hadn't made up my mind about us quite yet. We met briefly, and I painfully listened to the answers that I "so desperately" needed. Was I pretty enough? –"Of course, you are, I just wanted something different." Did I wait too long to give it up? –"No, not at all." Why her? –"She was different." (As if there's a perfect answer to that question). It didn't matter what he said, I already decided as soon as I saw him that I wanted him back. My instincts told me to brake, but I blindly kept going, thinking we were past our speed bumps and back in the traveling lane.

I forgot two important rules when traveling an accident-prone highway, however: 1) Proceed with caution and 2) Buckle-up! This time I wasn't as stunned. I noticed the warning signs and slowed down, but was still hit nonetheless. The signs read, "Fool me once" and "Fool me twice".

He was supposed to meet me one night for a date and never arrived. The next morning I called and texted him for answers, and once again, no response. I foolishly gave him the benefit of the doubt. Perhaps he was on his way and got into a car accident and that's why he wasn't answering his phone, I thought.

Through a friend, I discovered why he never showed up. He was on his way all right, but not to my house. The accident certainly didn't involve cars and that's why he wasn't answering his phone. According to the rumors, he ran back to his ex-girlfriend, yet again. What hurt most this time was being robbed of the last word. I didn't stall for too long though as I knew it would be ineffective for my progress. Dwelling on how I was going to tell him how much he hurt me again seemed futile. I therapeutically listened to Carrie Underwood's song, "Before He Cheats" on repeat for about two weeks, then decided to simply move on. I learned never to go down that road again and am proud to report I haven't seen him since. Afterward, I realized I depended too much on others to make me happy, and I had to set out by myself to make my own happiness.

Over time, I accepted the possibility of never knowing why. I didn't pursue answers because I didn't care for his reasons. I fixed most of the damage myself and kept going. Every day I got a little better. I started to become myself again, focusing only on good things to come. There were quick fixes to buffer out minor dents, but time is what really helped me. My bruised ego needed to heal on its own and moving forward was key. I believe everything happens for a reason and only time will truly tell. I knew something good was going to come from this and in several ways it has. Years later an opportunity presented itself which allowed me to finally have the last word, whether he knows it or not. After mulling it over, I asked myself, *is he really worth a second more of my time?* No, my story is through. Perhaps it will guide those traveling the same rocky path I once traveled.

When struck by life's unexpected roadblocks (which come in any form) it's important to look forward and turn negative experiences into positive actions. Using my past experience as the fuel to my future has driven me to great destinations. I have a new passenger, a map for my career path and a firm perspective on past relationships gone wrong. It's better to focus on the road ahead than to keep glaring in the rearview or, worse, do a U-turn.

****

Chaynna Campbell's work has previously been published in the Athol Daily: "The Power of Words" in dedication to Martin Luther King Jr., and "A Soldier's True Colors" as a tribute to our heroes. Chaynna is also an aspiring writer for children's books.

UNSHACKLE THE TRUTH
By Tina Jensen

It has been more than two and a half years. I still love you. It's obviously not that romantic kind of love or I would have left you shackled to your career without a second thought for the first, second or tenth guy who has passed my way since you left. Nor am I holding onto some remnant of hope that you will come back into my life; it's just that you have size ten feet and I've found no one to fill your shoes.

Besides. You are yourself. And I set you free.

Now I want to fill the void and unshackle my truth.

As much as the conspiracy theorists and seekers believe there are truths hidden in the shadows of the moon, I want you to know I love you.

No.

Like the sun warms the skin as it is set free holding hands with the early echoes of the world's awakening, I want you to feel I love you. Sometimes as subtle as the waft of a breeze as your lips grazed mine or as forceful as your 90 kilograms lifting me sky high and plunging me into the ocean, or carrying me up the stairs into your bed. I want you to feel this.

It's the kind of love where I loved and wanted all of you, just as you are. The bravery, timeless innocence, anxiety, ruggedness, flustered moods, intertwined hands, legs, lips and hearts, and other parts. Commitment, self-doubt, post-traumatic stress, generosity, bad dancing, a fierce intelligence that questioned everything yet accepted make-believe. Emotional voids, the ecstatic culmination of sleepless nights, everything you didn't tell me and everything for which you said "I'm sorry."

You are yourself. And I learned to let you be.

At 5 a.m. the bravery of an SAS soldier wanes as he calls out an SOS to help pack, not just one bag but an entire house. On the day the removalists are scheduled to remove all trace of a man about to embark on an underground mission, I arrive to a war zone of a flustered mind, lost control and not a trace of order. As I move from room to room, folding, rolling, hanging and wrapping each of your belongings carefully into suitcases and cartons, I recall the richness of our separate lives that twice had collided.

Early morning freezing ocean swims, dragging bedding to sleep by the fire on hardwood floors where a perfectly delicious bed was only meters away, having your rear end visually drag me around a lake inspiring me to not give up, teaching me the power of thinking about people who have inspired me as I swim laps, degustation dinners filling us with fine food, wine and yet another conversation that dragged into the wee hours, clapping out poetry rhythms, dodgem car rides at country shows inducing the inner ten year old's laughter, verbal transactions when you asked what God thought about those who kill people for a job. Yes, I heard, including the silence from the priest as his eyes turned downward and you walked away without any further words exchanged. Barefoot moonlight tiny dances and a touch that made my feet leave the earth only to land on a bed of clouds watching finger puppets on the ceiling whilst being serenaded by a wanna be Johnny Cash.

I remember running my index finger around the insignia of your brand new special services beret, knowing this meant goodbye. Knowing that as I forced you to leave your own home to get your toenails manicured, pick up your dry cleaning, your body massaged and your anxiety levels reduced, I may never do anything for, or with you, again.

Within the suitcases and cartons, I wrapped within your underwear and socks your deepest secrets that you hid so well from all around you and the memories of an unusually woven portrait of the oddest couple. One, motivated by a twenty year inheritance clause to become a highly ranked secret service operator in the depths of war zones fighting other people's battles and fending off moral injury with an armored shell that allows no emotions in. Rarely out. The other, determined to support others in their desire to battle their own internal wars, find justice from old pain and freedom from new heartaches by teaching them to let their emotions out.

And yet, as I shoved the edges of those boxes and suitcases as close together as I could to get them shut, I knew we worked. We managed to fit everything in. Everything together.

There have been many times since your "I am going to XXXX" text two and a half years ago that I've wanted to write and let you know I am thinking of you, wanting assurance you aren't one of the Australian SAS commandos currently in the Middle East's most harrowing of wars that has no end. Knowing that you are. Your face as you stoically told me you cannot think of anyone on a battlefield, for the life of yourself and your mates would be at risk. These things hold me back. And send me into the darkness where I let you free. Wanting to hold your face in my hands.

Reminded of you holding mine in yours, then turning to walk away with no last glance. Reminded as I watched the enormity of who and what was leaving my life continue to get smaller in the distance, the tears rolling down my cheeks were only of great respect and love. Not sadness.

I have often wondered if we had met years earlier would our connection have been the same? Would I have accepted someone into my life who was rarely there, needing proof of your love both in your physicality and your communication? Would you have loved me deeper if we had shared more time, trusting in the knowledge that I would not be curled up in a corner crying every day, hoping you were alive? Perhaps I would not have learned about the type of love that is not based on needs, allowing me to accept who you are and what you did, with neither attachment or expectation.

My thoughts shift to the future.

If we were only to meet on your return from Iraq, the influence of your commitment and determination to your long-term goals would not have made such an impact on my life during the two times we have connected. Despite your ability to find space to control your emotions and anxiety, there is no doubt any witnessing of atrocities will torment your future. As history shows, you will no longer be the man I love now. I simply cannot promise I could love the man you will become. For in the fortnightly stilted conversations with my Vietnam veteran father, I am reminded of what a soldier gives. And within the war zone jungle, loses.

Himself.

For who will you be, when you are no longer a soldier defined by your training and orders and your experience in the most harrowing of corners where the extremes of strength and fragility, death and heroism, collide?

It confuses and saddens me to think I may not love you if we were to meet for the first time during your darkest times.

And yet, how can I know who either of us will be in the future when so much time and experience will have passed? Will the thread that connected us for five and a half years still be strong or frayed by the continual harsh rubbings of life?

Right now, I cannot know, and so I make the choice to place the thread in my memory trunk to fade, never to be forgotten. Knowing as the sun and moon are so deeply connected, it is a thread that forms one of the boldest etchings within the tapestry of my life.

Time will continue to pass until your contract is completed. For my future's sake, I no longer can allow my life to stand still. I must set you free from my heart so love can once again shift inside me, instead of waiting for a droplet of your mind, body or soul to stir me. If in need on your return, I gift to you my promise to always be there for you. Because I know you trust me. And a soldier rarely trusts.

As I write this, I feel the heaviness of guilt. I am overwhelmed with deep sadness. I have thought about you every day for more than two and a half years and still recall vividly the smallest and heartiest connections we shared. As if they were happening now. I feel the dense inner turmoil of memories, not wanting to let you down, needing to know you are alive and wanting to hold your face in my hands.

Just one more time.

There is no doubt I love you deeply. And it is for this reason, within this chapter, I must let you go without a full stop, ensuring there is empty space to allow any future contact to complete the story.

I take a deep breath. As I release my love for you into the wind to let fly high within the Peruvian Andes, hummingbirds and dragonflies fly around me, embodying the spirit and energy you gave me.

Thank you for your gift of strength.

It is time for the blankness of a new page to open.

Unshackle the heart

Like the moon sets the sun free

To become itself

****

Tina Jensen is a world traveler, wellness coach and kindle of www.createnoordinarylife.com, a movement borne from the need to be inspired, passionate, challenged and satisfied. She is full of ideas, feelings and experiences and can often be found simply being still. She sees the world through a kaleidoscopic lens of experience, empathy and awe. Tina is passionate about sharing real stories of ordinary people committed to the pursuit of dreams, extinguishing the mundane, overcoming challenges and feeling compelled to make a difference, either to their own lives or those of others. She simply wants you to say yes.

ONE SHORT DAY IN THE EMERALD CITY
By Maeve Corbett

It was the summer of 1967 and my parents had taken my best friend and me to Disneyland, The Happiest Place on Earth.

The label "best friend", of course, suggests reciprocal feelings. From the first moment I met her in high school the previous September, she was someone who was impossible to look away from.

"Ugh," I'd thought at first. She was one of the popular people, someone who had seemingly never been called upon to develop anything more complex than a dazzling smile and perfect hair.

"Ugh," she'd probably thought at first about me. I was quiet and brainy and may as well have had a green complexion for as badly as I fit in with the beautiful people who comprised her circle of A-list friends.

I didn't have a name for it at the time but, in retrospect, I was clearly an Elphaba to her Glinda. Things came easily to her because she projected such radiance and I was fairly certain that there wasn't a single boy on the entire campus who wasn't madly in love with her. I subconsciously set out to dislike her because she represented everything I felt was superficial in the world.

Yet as the saying goes that the line between love and hate is much thinner than we'd like to imagine, I secretly couldn't help but wonder what it might be like to walk for a day in her shoes and to be the person whose name was spoken in awe on so many pairs of lips.

I don't remember exactly when our friendship began. Maybe it was simply that Fate had conspired to throw us into so many of the same classes together our first semester. "Here we are again," she had remarked with a smile. The fact she learned my name before I learned hers felt unusual at the time. Who was I, after all, but a plain girl who studied hard, who wore clothes that my mother picked out, and who belonged to geeky groups like the chess club? Someone like her, I thought, was beyond comprehending the dreams I had to one day create magic through the power of music. Someone like her, I thought, had no need to expend energy on a golden future because she was already enjoying such a sparkling existence in the present without lifting a finger.

On the surface, the two of us had nothing in common with one another and it, thus, always amazed me on the occasions when we'd accidentally fall in step together between classes and start talking and laughing as if we had known each other all our lives.

I remember glancing around and hoping others would see us – not just the popular kids who might look beyond my being different but also the other kids like myself who might feel a smidge of envy I had somehow crossed a mysterious boundary and been transformed. Little by little, hers became the approval I wanted to have, the seal of confirmation that maybe I wasn't such an ugly duckling after all.

When my parents asked me if I wanted to take a friend to Disneyland, I didn't hesitate a moment in telling them who it would be. Two friends – two best friends – having the time of their lives in a place built on dreams and possibilities and that enjoyed no interference from the outside world – who could want for more?

Little did I know I'd be sitting in the audience at a Broadway show 40 years later watching *Wicked* and feeling such a profound pang of sadness. One short day in the Emerald City isn't nearly enough when there is still so much that has yet to be said.

The seduction of popularity can be a cruelty beyond definition. For the four years we were together in high school, I never did breach the walls that socially divided us, much less been invited in through the front door. The two of us could talk for hours on the phone on summer afternoons about our dysfunctional families but, come September again, hers was a world where beauty and popularity clearly reigned and the most I could ever hope for were occasional glimpses from afar. She was still my best friend and yet her own best friends were everyone except me.

We stayed in touch for a time after graduation, a time in which I began to vigorously pursue my career as a concert pianist and, in the words of Elphaba, to defy gravity and not let anyone pull me down. I like to think she was happy for me, though I'm sure the subtle reversal in our positions was confusing. I was finally getting the attention and hearing the applause I had so hungrily craved in my youth (and all those days of practice, practice, practice!) and yet the distance between us continued to widen.

Why was it, I wondered, that I was the one getting exactly the life I had always thought should have been hers for the taking?

There's a fragile moment in the second act of *Wicked* in which both women realize that there is no turning back. It could easily be the two of us standing on that stage and being unable to put into words how we wish things could be different and that our respective worlds could co-exist. My own Glinda may not have remained in Oz as its reigning queen of goodness but her marriage to a man who speaks for God from a pulpit probably ranks a close second.

I wanted to be happy for her choice in spite of the fact that he clearly held me in little regard and might have snatched up the nearest pail of water if he'd thought it would really work in permanently dispatching me from her life.

Was it because I was one of those crazy New Yorkers who hung around with artists, musicians and poets? Was it because he knew that a religion which deemed women to be subservient wasn't one I could warm to? Or was it just because I'd known her much longer than he did and his own insecurities compelled him to wield a virtual eraser?

I remember commenting a few days before her wedding that I'd never have thought a homecoming queen would end up with a minister. The outgoing personality and glamour that had been the trademark of who she was to so many of us had become – in the matter of a few short months – absorbed to the point of vanishing altogether. With a smile that implored me to understand, she replied that she liked being a part of something that was so pure and so good and that she was marrying a man whose word was being followed by a lot of people.

"You could belong there, too," she said, "and then we'd see each other all the time." The only tradeoff, I realized, would be to abandon my ambition to be an instrument of change and to docilely accept, as she did, that being an obedient follower was the "right" thing for a woman to do.

Nearly a quarter of a century would pass before we'd be in contact again. When a mutual friend provided me with her email address, I was initially euphoric. "I've missed you so much," she wrote back. "We have lots to catch up on!" She asked me if I remembered all the fun we had at Disneyland. That it was the first memory she associated with our friendship gladdened my heart.

The stream of correspondence I hoped would ensue, however, was sporadic. I recall her surprise that I remembered her birthday after the passage of so many years. "You'll have to remind me when yours is," she insisted and yet no cards ever followed as a result of my telling her that it is – and always has been – exactly two months before hers. My loving husband asks me why the acknowledgment of someone who has spent more time out of my life than actually in it should still continue to matter. In honesty, I don't have an answer. People come in and out of our lives and the length of their stay isn't something within our control. We grow up. We grow apart. We grow to see that sometimes the things we want the most dearly come at a cost we could not have anticipated.

And yet — because they were the very first to define what we wanted a best friend to be - we never forget them, no matter how many new friends cross our paths in the course of a lifetime and lay potential claim to the title.

****

A classically trained musician, Maeve Corbett has played with symphonies around the world as well as recorded soundtracks for independent films. Though she is now semi-retired, music continues to be a staple in the Cotswald cottage she shares with her husband, three dogs and a South American parrot with a sailor's salty vocabulary and an attitude to match.

THE STING OF REGRET
By Johanna Baker-Dowdell

Regret. Just six letters, but when put together in that word those six letters summon up layer upon layer of heartache and what ifs and I wishes. But the biggest regret is that I'll never know what could have been, and all because I wasn't brave.

I've always thought workplace romances a bit cliché, but that was because I had never been presented with an attractive option. Until Anthony. I was his team leader and he was one of three new recruits who started on the same day. Over the next few weeks I trained my new team members in our customer service systems, concentrating on the areas with which they needed help.

It wasn't until my boss commented on Anthony being, "the ugliest man alive," that I thought about him in any way beyond strictly a members of my team. I was surprised by my instant defensive reaction to the comment, and found myself silently listing Anthony's attractive qualities in a way that showed my subconscious had been busy considering him without me noticing.

Suddenly I was looking at a smile that took in his entire face, his eyes creasing at the edges to form crinkles that told the story of much happiness. And I was noticing the easy way he spoke with other members of our team, gently teasing each of us with insightful comments. I let that thought sit with me and moved on with the rest of the work day.

Within weeks Anthony and I had become firm friends. He often texted me when he was taking a break, eager to chat with me about whatever was on his mind that day. I welcomed this, as most of my friends were still in Australia; England could be lonely for a woman reliant on an alcoholic husband for support.

It was during these lunchtime conversations that Anthony spoke about the older brother whom he admired, a stepfather he respected greatly and a mother he adored. He bought a calling card specifically to speak with his mum, telling her his news every night after he got home from work and just as she woke up in Australia. When he was feeling down he summoned his mum's voice in his head, telling him to keep up the "positive mental attitude." I could have used a chat with Anthony's mum from time to time myself.

But this friendship wasn't all one-sided listening on my part. Anthony provided a willing ear when things with my emotionally absent husband went awry, which was often. Unlike most men, Anthony didn't try to fix the situation; he just listened and answered only when asked a specific question. I spent a lot of time working through my marital issues, but it was a nice change to have someone who knew what was happening behind my cheery façade.

As the crisp English autumn days got shorter and frost started to knock on our doors each morning, I was told our team would be travelling to Scotland for work. As a mobile customer service team we already traversed the country every second week, but this time we would be spending three weeks away and returning right before Christmas. Time away was a welcome distraction as the situation in my marriage became tenuous. I packed all my warm clothes, my favorite books and my courage as I embarked on a trip that would see me spending three weeks with just my male workmates for company.

Leaving early one Sunday morning, my suitcase packed and anticipation high, I kissed my husband goodbye and drove to pick up the three men who made up my team. The green hills of England's midlands gave way to the hilly northern counties and as twilight fell we crossed the border to Scotland. We were excited about what was ahead, the new places we would visit and the chance to get away from our day-to-day lives for a time.

I had a close team and we enjoyed each other's company, so we fell easily into a routine that saw us meeting for work in the hotel foyer each morning, completing the day's door-to-door calls, eating dinner together and then relaxing in the room Anthony and his two teammates shared, watching TV or DVDs together. Quite often Anthony and I sat together on his bed chatting and every so often he would tickle me until I was reduced to hysterical laughter.

Late one night as I watched TV in my own room, I heard a slight knock at the door and wondered who it could be. Hesitating momentarily, I thought it might be someone from the hotel reception coming to speak to me about one of my team members. Embarrassed to be answering the door in my pajamas, I grabbed a long-sleeved t-shirt to cover my body in lieu of a robe.

I grasped the door handle and opened it just enough to see who was knocking, expecting to see a bored, uniformed figure in front of me. Instead it was Anthony, standing confidently in the doorway, his skinny, lanky frame filling the space. My embarrassment quickly turned to horror as I considered what to do. We had been flirting for weeks, edging around a growing attraction but neither voicing what we were feeling.

Unsure how to react and horrified he was seeing me this way - hair messy, braless and completely slovenly - I ushered him in quickly, giving him a quizzical look as I did. He walked straight across the room and stretched out on my bed, looking very settled.

"Um, hi. Is everything ok?" I questioned.

"Why wouldn't it be?" Anthony said, and I saw the creases forming at the side of his eyes. "I just wanted to see how you were."

"Well you've seen now," I said nervously, instinctively trying to cover myself.

"Come and sit down. I want to chat," he said, patting the space on the bed next to where he was lounging.

As I approached the bed awkwardly, he straightened up and grabbed the hairbrush that was sitting on the table next to my bed.

"I want to brush your hair," he said matter-of-factly.

He motioned for me to sit in the space in front of him, spreading his legs apart so I could sit closer.

My back rigidly straight and every muscle tense, I sat silently in front of Anthony. I could hear him breathing behind me as my mind raced, thinking of all the possible ways this scene could play out. Anthony started brushing my long brown hair slowly, methodically, sensuously, and I willed my mind to quiet, trying to enjoy the experience with a man I was attracted to both mentally and physically.

He held my hair gently between his long, thin fingers and brushed sections at a time, starting at the ends and working his way up to the roots. I relaxed into his body, wiggling backwards so I could get closer to him, smelling his musky odor as I closed my eyes. But I could not let myself go completely. As comfortable as I felt in that moment, what could have been a blissful experience was taunted by questions of fidelity and fear of what he would think of my body. I could sense him willing me to surrender, and I almost did.

Suddenly he dropped the brush and stood, grazing his hands across the front of his jeans as he moved. Without a sound he strode across the room, opened the door and left, leaving me sitting open-mouthed in stunned silence. Annoyed at myself for letting that chance slip through my fingers, I spent a sleepless night alternating between willing myself to act on my instincts if I was presented with the opportunity again and berating myself for almost being unfaithful.

Our potential relationship simmered for the remaining two weeks of our work trip, but almost boiled over as Anthony stayed with us over Christmas while waiting to find somewhere new to live in London. Every night I climbed the stairs to the bedroom I shared with my husband, wondering how long it would take me to calm my thoughts and, if I did sleep, what my dreams would contain as Anthony slept on our lounge below.

As New Year's Eve approached, Anthony left for his new address and my life returned to normal. I was exhausted by the will we/won't we scenario I constantly reviewed in my head, but satisfied I'd stayed true to my vows. The New Year heralded my new resolve to commit to my marriage and my husband seemed to share that resolution. We started planning a six-week trip to Turkey and Greece after Easter and Anthony and I returned to our platonic lunchtime chats.

As I prepared dinner after work one evening, my phone rang on the bench next to me. I saw it was Anthony calling and assumed he must have left something in the work car and wanted me to check. I answered the phone playfully, ready to tease him. Instead of replying with his usual light-hearted banter, the voice I heard was serious. Anthony explained he wouldn't be at work the next day, or for the near future. His words cracked and I could hear the tears choking in his throat. His stepfather had died that morning – a massive heart attack that took his life instantly – and he was in a taxi on the way to Heathrow Airport to catch a plane to Melbourne for his funeral.

My heart jumped and a surge of emotion heated my body. He was grief-stricken and I wanted to hug him, to show him I cared. I quickly told him to let me know if there was anything I could do. He thanked me and hung up.

Over the next fortnight we texted and emailed as he filled me in on how he and his family were and what was happening in the aftermath of his stepfather's death. One text read, "Coming back soon. Keep my job open for me?" his tone light, as usual. I was thrilled at the thought of seeing him again soon and I knew we had crossed into a deeper relationship. I had to consider how I would handle his return.

The following week I sent a text asking which day he would arrive in London and telling him I hoped I wouldn't miss him as I was flying to Istanbul the following weekend. He didn't respond and, although disappointed, I busied myself with preparations for my impending trip. I assumed I would catch up with him when I returned from Greece.

Three weeks later as I waited at Rhodes port for the ferry to Naxos my phone rang. It was Anthony! I told my husband I was going to look at the water and then answered it when I was a safe distance away.

"Hi Anthony! Are you back?" I said excitedly.

"Hello, is this Johanna?" a female voice asked tentatively, and my elation faded.

"This is Maureen, Anthony's mother. I'm afraid I have some bad news," the woman said, her voice faltering.

"Anthony died. It's taken me several weeks to work up the courage to call you and let you know," she said.

"But why? How did this happen? He's only 25," my words tumbled, as confusion, anger and sadness all fought to envelope me.

"He died in his sleep. They're still trying to find the exact cause."

"Oh," a tiny sound was all I could muster as I struggled to take this news in.

"Anthony spoke about you all the time so I wanted to let you know personally," Maureen said.

"Thanks. I'm so sorry for your loss," I mumbled.

"Thank you Johanna. Goodbye."

Regret had already pierced me but as I played that conversation over and over in my mind, it wound its fingers tightly around my heart.

****

Johanna Baker-Dowdell is a fiction and nonfiction author, journalist, blogger, PR consultant and PhD candidate, studying the way newspaper journalists use social media texts to report on crisis events. Johanna owns writing and public relations consultancy Strawberry Communications, which generates publicity for small and medium businesses internationally. In her down time, she enjoys writing, reading baking sweet treats, travel and walking.

BASEBALL AND TREASURE CHESTS
By Rachael Protzman Hardman

I'm the kind of girl who says it like it is. I can be gentle and subtle. Sometimes. But, mostly, I have no qualms about giving my opinion. I'm also very open. I have to censor myself at times, reminding myself that not everyone is so comfortable with certain topics. In my older age, I like to think that I've developed some grace when it comes to opening my mouth. Maybe.

So, how did I get that way? I'm not really sure. You see, my mother is a strong woman, for sure. But, not as confident as I am. She probably realizes that not everyone cares to hear her opinion. Or maybe she isn't as sure of herself. I'm not quite certain. But, my dad. There's the real confusion. You see, getting him to open up is like trying to pry open a 400-year-old treasure chest that was buried beneath the ocean and then dragged to shore and allowed to rust for another 100 years.

I love my dad. But sometimes, I feel like I don't know him. As a child and through my teen years, he was in my life through softball. Baseball was his thing, still is. And he feels comfortable connecting through it. I kept playing because I didn't want to lose him. He didn't know how to connect to or talk to a 13-year-old girl full of raging emotions and hormones. So, softball was it. He coached, I played. I wasn't always the best player, but damn, I tried hard and I sure as hell never gave up. And I saw the pride in him. He could talk to me about the game, about my performance, about my team, the other team, the other coaches, the other players and on and on and on.

Despite his faults, my dad always encouraged me. And I am grateful for that. I never once doubted that I could do something. I still don't. I make shit happen. And my father is proud of me for this. I don't know that because he told me. He never sat down and said, "Hey kid, sky's the limit and you can do anything, I know you can because I see it in you." No. I know he's proud of me because one of his favorite stories to tell is how my high school coach once commented that just when he thought I reached my maximum potential, I got better. He likes that story so much he included it in his toast at my wedding.

Then there's the story I've heard over and over. Of his two girls on the field in a high school game, one at the pitcher's mound and one at first base. My sister scooped up a ground ball and instead of gently throwing it to me at first base to get the runner out, she waited. Messing with the runner. Then she whipped it to me at the last second. I was pissed and yelled at her for screwing around. We screamed at each other in the middle of the game, spectators laughing at the obvious sibling rivalry. I stand by that to this day. She shouldn't have waited. An out wasn't worth that. But, when Dad tells the story, you can hear the humor in his voice, and behind that, the pride. He was proud of her spunk, her sass. He was proud to have his two girls, personalities as different as night and day, standing up to each other over a play in the middle of a game.

That's just Dad's way. He can say the words "I'm proud of you." He can say "I love you." And he does. But, he prefers to say it with a story. Ideally, a baseball story.

But, what about him? I have had so many questions over the years. What was life like for him growing up? Who were his parents, what were they like? His father died before I was born, when my dad was in his early 20s. And, I know very little about the man who was my grandfather. Little snippets, here and there. What was my father like as a kid, a teenager, a college student? What in his life is he proud of? Ashamed of? How did he become the man he is today? So many unanswered questions. A story here, a story there. But, never really answers.

Thing is, I'm no longer a 13-year-old or even 18-year-old girl full of raging emotions and hormones, someone with whom it is difficult to communicate or connect. I got older and stopped playing softball after high school. And still, I struggle to connect with dad. There are still lots of softball memories for dad to talk about. And talk about. And talk about. And, now we talk about my kids and his writing. But, where is he in all of this? Where is the man who is my dad?

I learn more about my dad by reading his stories than by talking to him. And this used to break my heart. I have tried to pry open the treasure chest. Asked about his childhood, his parents, his brothers. But, I can tell he doesn't like to talk about it. Maybe it's too painful. Maybe he's in denial. Maybe he just doesn't understand how much I want to know, how much I feel like I don't know about him. Whatever it is that makes him not talk, I've come to realize, it's ok. My dad loves me in the way he knows how. Through baseball or softball, through loving my kids, through writing. And I love him back. Even though he is far from perfect.

I used to have an idea in my head of what love looks like and how it is shown. A very specific idea. In letting go of that ideal, I've come to understand my father in a different way. He's human. And because he is human, he isn't going to be perfect, to love me in the way that I think is perfect. He's going to love me in the way that he knows how. I'm not sure exactly when the light bulb went on. But, since realizing that my father is actually a human being with his own emotions and ways of expressing them, I feel as though I am able to have a better relationship with him. I'm able to accept him for who he is and accept his love for how he can give it. Not how I think it should be done. In the end, my father reaches out through sharing something he loves, baseball. And, despite the questions that still exist, that is enough for me.

My unfinished chapter is that I don't know his life, his experiences, good or bad. Heroic or shameful. And, yes, that makes me sad. As I said, it used to break my heart. Used to. Not anymore. At least, not much anymore. Because, I've grown up enough to realize that love doesn't always mean knowing someone's story. Love means knowing, under all that hard shell exterior, knowing someone's heart. Knowing they love you in the way they know how, to the best of their abilities. For me, love means understanding that sometimes a story about baseball is not just a story about baseball.

****

Rachael Protzman Hardman is a 2003 graduate of the University of Notre Dame. She spent 10 years working in the field of journalism as a reporter, editor and page designer. In addition, she rewrote and edited a book that was recently published. She currently works at her home in Ohio with her husband and two young children.

LOOK TO THE OTTOMAN
By Marnie Macauley

On August 4th my husband of 30 years, Ian, had a devastating stroke. I found him wedged between two kitchen cabinets. He couldn't get up, nor could I lift him. At first I thought he'd tripped. It quickly became clear that something horrific had happened.

I called 911, then ran back to him.

In that moment, we both felt it might be our last together. Through tears, we spoke the words that had been silent between us for far too long.

Our marriage hasn't been idyllic. But, much like the Cyclone at Coney Island, the highs were thrilling. On top, it's been a heady journey with this brilliant former The New York Times senior editor, who opened up the world to me; a world of scholars, actors, and Nobel Laureates. It was Ian who encouraged me to write, and edited my early pieces. Somehow, we made it through without divorce or serious bodily injury. His genius as an editor was in two deceptively simple principles: "If it ain't broke, don't futz with it." and "You're a writer if somebody pays you!"

And now this lifelong wordsmith was struck down. He's lost the use of his left side, his speech is slurred, and there are blood pressure, and swallowing issues. For those who have been through something similar, you know. You know the fear, the horrific insult to the body, and most of all, that life will be forever changed.

He's currently in a fourth rehab, and then his insurance for in-house is questionable. I'll bring him home if I have to carry him on my back. (Massage offers, welcome.)

I've been through devastating tragedy before and know that these times shadow you forever. The thoughts, feelings, fears, are easily re-triggered with each new crisis. Yes, they can weaken the soul, but they can also strengthen, providing they're met with optimism, determination, the ability to major multi-task at warp speed – and yes, humor.

"Humor?" "Stroke?" For those who pooh-pooh Jewish humor, I promise you, it's not only alive, it can keep you alive. It's even "catching."

There are now hospital staff, from African-Americans to Filipinos, saying "Oy vey!" when he swallows wrong, and "chutzpah" a lot - usually about me.

CASE MANAGER: "Well, he's not making the progress we'd hoped for, so ... "

ME: "Sweetheart, I'm deaf, he can't speak! Finally, a perfect match! Ah, but he's an editor, so, how about we get him into the best next rehab and work on his criticism skill. Trust me, he'll correct a parrot."

I'm up to three shows a day. I'm thinking of taking it on the road: "'Stroking' on Your Summer Vacation!"

I'd open with Medicare. I've learned when you've had a stroke on Medicare you're suddenly Mr. Popularity. At the first place, a lady visited to make short-term rehab plans at her facility. But wait ... there's more. Next, a chipper fellow with teeth like piano keys and a brochure that resembled the Ritz bopped in. It seems Medicare pays them $140 a day, so the competition makes *Survivor* contestants look like they're in a coma. At his place, Ian would be surrounded by antiques (faux), satellite TV (which no one could operate), a fridge that fit nothing, and cute "activities" like "let's-do-our-nails-Wednesday." So there he went. Finding an empty glass, however, was a problem they hadn't yet licked.

For this you need more than humor. I found that hysteria helps. On a particular Thursday night, a lovely Filipino CNA, asked me in broken English: "Can Jews take shower on Thursday?"

ME: "Wha ...? Back up Rena, what are you talking about?"

HER: "Well, Monday, he say 'Jews can no take showers on Monday.'"

ME: "Who said?"

HER: "Yo husband say 'Jews no take showers on Mondays. So Thursday OK for Jew?"

He can barely talk or swallow, yet in this new "world according to Ian" (who doesn't want to be dragged to a wheelchair, then a tiny room of pouring water), Jews can't shower on Mondays. I saw his lip curl.

"You couldn't have at least chosen the Sabbath?!" I asked, laughing. I suggested that staff run his 'religious reasons' by me in the future.

Driving. Magellan, I'm not. As soon as someone says: "Go South on I-95, make a U-turn at the Interstate ..." I start humming the theme from *Jeopardy*! When Ian had to be transferred yet again, I was told Medicare doesn't cover it. I suppose the Feds expect the "stroke stork" to "beak" them down from hospital to hospital. So, I bravely decided to take him myself. Picture it: wheel chair, catheter, and a 140 pound man who can't walk or hold his head upright and can barely talk.

On the ten minute ride, there was Ian, strapped in next to me – pointing at a stop sign a mile away. As usual he was directing my driving! Naturally, I couldn't find the right entrance. I said, "Don't worry, we'll find it soon," to which he replied, quite clearly: "No we won't."

Another "positive" is, I've lost 25 pounds, can lift a Hummer, and could enter NASCAR as a human vehicle. This, from a woman who, on August 4th, assumed only two positions: lying and sitting. The next day, I revved from zero to 100, rising at dawn, unpacking our new apartment including 5,000 books, running to the hospital, learning occupational therapy, speech therapy, and yes, automotive maintenance.

I call it "The Stroke Diet." I'd take it public but it still has a few kinks.

Ask any of "us" relatives of stroke victims. We can tell who we are. We're the ones wearing our clothes inside out, who alternate from hyper mania to depression with fusilli-gone-wild do's. (Finally, a nurse "dreadlocked" me.) In this small private world we bond instantly. One Black mom, Doris, (whose son had a stroke), and I fell into each other's arms. As we compared notes, we laughed and cried together, sharing peeves. For example, she said her sister told her: "If only he'd exercised, ate healthy, and taken better care of himself." My neighbor suggested my husband be given a) 10,000 units of Vitamin C; b) canned asparagus; and c) buy the herbals he recommended four months ago. What can you say? "Because I'm a lousy wife who denied him 'cures'-by-idiots?" How about "You knew it was coming. You were at least prepared." We laughed, sadly, knowingly. All we wanted to hear was: "How can I help?" Yes, we were frightened to our core. Her final comment? "We're gonna live a long time, honey." Why? At the same time, we both said simply: "Because we have to."

Not a day goes by when I don't think about the women who have gone through unimaginable pain and loss especially during the Holocaust, 9-11 and other atrocities. I take enormous comfort from them. If they could endure torture, the camps, gas chambers, the huge sudden insane loss, then this, I've decided, must be a cakewalk. Every moment I feel their loving arms around me, and hear their words: "Do what you must. One step at a time. Because you have to."

The other day I bought an ottoman on local webcam E-bay Channel 108. What a find! A 50 pound, used, leather ottoman for storage which could double as a much-needed table, for 15 bucks!

One of my mama muses tapped me on the shoulder, saying: "Bring it to the hospital. Show Ian. Show him … the future. That you believe in the future, with him home. A future with new understanding and promise between you."

So I dragged our ottoman the mile from the car to the hospital (sitting on it every 30 feet). I've been known to be quirky, but a woman, clothes inside out, with half a head of dreadlocks holding a massive round ottoman, was, as one doctor put it: "A first."

Ian liked the ottoman. I went on to describe "the deal," where we'd put it, etc.

I don't know what the future will hold. But now I "Look to the ottoman!" The way I figure, life's a lot like that. A bit worn sometimes, a bit frayed ... but built of precious material. And oh, the capacity for beauty, that has been, and God willing, is still to be stored!

Epilogue: Ian died 10 months later in my arms. I've always loathed the word "widow." Widows are spiders, black widows, Queen Victoria in perpetual black, shrouded mourning. Yes, we all grieve uniquely. For this "widow," the most helpful words aren't those describing what could've, should've, might've been. When I look to the ottoman, I'm reminded that regardless of what the future brings, I was, and always will be - a wife.

****

Quirky, no-nonsense, funny Marnie Macauley - award-winning writer, editor, author, lecturer, clinician, and administrator - is a straight-shooter who has a distinctive voice and takes on the world in her columns, features, and books. Ms. Macauley has written more than 20 books/calendars. She has been nominated for both an Emmy and Writers Guild award. She was also chosen as a Distinguished Woman in Las Vegas in March of 2014. Join her on Facebook, LinkedIn, and Twitter. Website: www.marniemacauley.com. Email: asksadie@aol.com. For counseling, she can be reached at Liveperson: http://www.prestoexperts.com. (Click on the Counseling tab and type her name.)

THIEVES OF TIME
By Rachel McGrath

I quickly plunged myself behind a thick hedging bush. I held my breath and my heart pulsed as I panicked that she had seen me. My body held rigid, and I vainly hoped that she would walk straight past, no suspicion at all, giving me sense of déjà vu.

Rewind thirty years and I had hidden from this same person within another hedge, playing a game of hide-and-seek. Back then my concealment was in fun and jest, followed by 'I found you!' squeals of laughter and games of chase. I was only eight years old back then and the world seemed so immense, with only daydreams of the future. My only motivation at that time was to complete my homework before sundown so I could enjoy time with my friends.

At that age, friendships were crucial, and hours were spent on cliques, sports, the latest fad and holidays. Looking back it seemed such a simple lifestyle. Nonetheless, to a young girl it was an intense competition for popularity and social acceptance; both critical within a highly political school system. I don't recall thinking much on these matters, and when friendships were tested, they never seemed to expire quickly. As kids we would often bicker, snub or gossip around each other, and yet before long we would be exchanging clothes, braiding hair or finding new 'crushes' to spy upon; and all was forgiven. Disagreements were forgotten as the new fad was found, and friendships mended over days; sometimes hours.

This woman, Anna, her friendship was unique. We didn't go to the same school; we didn't even live in the same suburb. Anna lived with her father, and we were introduced through her aunt, who lived on my street. Anna would stay with her aunt throughout the school holidays. I recall that we first met at a neighborhood barbeque, with many of the local families and their children. At first, Anna had been a little wary, staying by her aunt's side as she clearly did not know anyone and she seemed uncomfortable in that loud and raucous setting.

Kids, however, are not shy, and we soon convinced Anna to play a game of tag and join our fun. Before long, we had become good friends, and it became a custom for Anna to stay with her aunt during the school holidays. Holiday breaks became even more appealing, as Anna and I would spend entire days together playing, and sometimes evenings over dinner and board games. We were inseparable, yet during the school term we rarely spoke or wrote to each other. There was a mutual acknowledgment of our friendship, and we would both eagerly be waiting for the next term holiday with anticipation.

Anna had a tough upbringing; her mother was an abusive alcoholic who left when she very young. Whilst she never shared the entire story, I could always tell that there was something missing, and she longed for that maternal support. I could not fathom this, having parents who were strict but always kind. Whilst her aunt was dependable and patient, she could never replace a mother, and Anna was only with her a few weeks every year. Her father was also a good man who clearly loved Anna immensely. He worked long hours to keep her clothed, fed and educated, and he did his absolute best to provide structure and discipline. Nonetheless, I always felt the memory of her mother seemed to haunt Anna's dark brown eyes.

As we grew into our early teens I sensed that the gap Anna's mother had left was growing larger. Whilst I didn't attend her school, and our friendship was tied to several weeks over each school holiday, I observed a difference in Anna's behavior as time passed. She started to dress a little more provocatively, experimenting with make-up and even carrying a packet of cigarettes in her bag. There were other subtle changes, such as her taste in music and the way she spoke about her school friends and interests. Regardless, we didn't change and we carried on our tradition every school holiday, making the most of the time we got to spend together.

I recall the year I turned fifteen, waiting for Anna's arrival at the start of the holidays, lingering on my front porch, and watching for her dad's car to arrive, excitedly waiting! When Anna had not yet arrived three days later, I was becoming anxious and counseled myself to enquire directly with her aunt. Arriving at the front door, Anna's aunt greeted me with trepidation; the look on her face told me she was dreading my arrival. She informed me that Anna would not be visiting these holidays at all, and told me to go and enjoy the sunshine. I left confused, hurt that she hadn't arrived, unsure if anything was wrong. My paranoia set in with questions over the future of our friendship. Would I see Anna again?

I left to sulk on my front porch, feeling directionless and dejected by the news that I would not see my friend for another entire semester. My mother found me wallowing in self-pity later that day as she had heard about Anna's non-arrival. She quietly entrusted me with information that Anna had been caught shoplifting and was in trouble with the police. She had been running with a disruptive crowd, and her father had found drugs in her bedroom. In punishment, she was confined to stay home for the holiday to catch up on her schoolwork. This news truly shocked me!

Of course I had realized Anna had changed over the years, but at the heart of it, we were always the same silly girls who giggled our way through each summer. I felt saddened that she may be alone right now! Although I made the most of the remaining holidays, I often thought of Anna's predicament and I stewed about what she may be feeling or thinking. Would she continue down this path or would she take the punishment and change? I also contemplated our friendship, worried that I may be too boring for her now, thinking she may not feel our holidays would be exciting enough for her now.

I didn't contact Anna directly as it would have seemed strange after so many years to telephone when we had never conversed between holidays before. Truthfully, I didn't even know her phone number and asking for it would perhaps make her embarrassed about what had happened.

Throughout the school term, I'd often catch myself thinking about Anna and wishing for the holidays to arrive quickly. I needed reassurance that she was okay and I also felt nervous about our friendship. Thoughts that Anna may not want to return to her aunt's home in the coming holidays kept troubling me.

My worries subsided as the holidays arrived and Anna promptly knocked on my front door. We hugged and laughed, and time stood still once more. I noticed this time that Anna's appearance was significantly different from my own plain, sensible attire, but that alone made no difference to our friendship. Anna never spoke to me about what had happened and I didn't ask. From my perspective it didn't matter as I was truly glad to have my friend back.

Like many teenage girls, my priorities were changing, and life was suddenly all about exams, boys, fashion and angst for the future. The year I turned seventeen and school assignments were complete, I just wanted to party! With holidays starting, and many school friends arranging 'end of exam' celebrations, I hoped that Anna would also want to join such revelries.

The first night she arrived, Anna readily agreed to come to a party, following me and the loud music to a friend's house where naturally there was underage drinking and young couples finding dark corners. I swiftly veered us towards my group of school friends, and with them in the circle was my latest crush, a boy in my year, Scott; someone I had bashfully pursued from a distance. Anna was confident, she was funny, and I could tell Scott took to her immediately. I tried to concentrate on the group's conversation, but my pulse raced as I watched Anna and Scott casually flirt the night through. I had never told her of my feelings for Scott. I had told no one! Therefore, I had no reason to blame her for taking advantage. Strangely however, I felt betrayed.

As the night progressed, I reconciled that nothing could come of this. Anna lived more than an hour away, and surely both would foresee any relationship as unfeasible. Yet as we left the party, I overheard Anna agreeing to a 'date'; movie and dinner later that week. Devastated doesn't even start to describe my emotions at that moment.

Anna bubbled all the way home, oblivious to my somber mood, and as the week led on, I felt I was the one seeking Anna out for time. Often I would interrupt phone calls with Scott; me the silent companion just listening to hours of their excited conversations. Following their date, I felt the situation had become far worse and Scott started hanging out with us - at my house! I wanted to scream at them both, but what could I do? I chastised myself for not speaking up sooner, as now these two, my friend and my crush were canoodling together in front of my eyes. It was beyond bearable.

Finally Anna sensed the friction growing, and questioned me. I became irrational, emotional and suddenly all of that angst I was feeling came pouring out. I felt she had intruded on my territory, and I was insanely jealous that Scott seemed so enamored with her. The exchange did not end well, it was never going to. She was upset but barely responded to my outburst. She left me there, and stalked back to her aunt's home in anger. We didn't speak to each other again. Through the rest of the holidays I could only watch from afar, seeing her come and go with Scott, and it was like I never existed.

At that time I was furious, green with envy and undeniably upset. I had lost a good friend and I was too obstinate to fix it. The day Anna left, I miserably watched her dad arrive to collect her. I hoped that she would come to see me, but both of us were being stubborn and neither gave in. Scott was there too, seeing her off, and that itself made me more willful in my scorn.

Anna didn't return the following holidays and I graduated from school soon afterward, heading onto university. I had heard that Anna and Scott broke-up soon after and my interest in Scott actually had waned by that point. I'm unsure if he ever knew that he caused the rift in our precious friendship.

Today, crouching behind this hedge, those memories came flooding back. Time stood still, and a part of me wanted to jump out and greet her, forgetting the years that had passed. Alas, the sensible side of me felt that any encounter would make for an uncomfortable and awkward reception. Shameful, I bent out of sight and waited for her footsteps to fade. I emerged slowly from hiding, looking around should anyone have noticed my humiliating cowardice. I composed myself and searched for Anna, catching sight as she turned the street corner; stepping out of my life once more.

Reflecting on our friendship, I wished to return to a time when Anna and I would laugh and play with no cares in the world. Perhaps today we are different people with little in common. Nonetheless, at one time our connection was strong and I now felt remorseful that petty teenage angst became the breaking point for our friendship, letting emotions overrule our sensibility. Regrets aside, that friendship provided some of the happiest times in my childhood, and those memories will live on forever. Smiling, I walked the other way.

****

Rachel McGrath grew up in Australia, where she studied before moving to the United Kingdom in her early thirties. She currently lives near London. She has always had a passion for writing both fiction and nonfiction and she has only recently published her first work, "Finding the Rainbow," a personal memoir. Rachel has also started blogging, specifically on her own fertility journey, a subject she feels is not openly talked about, and she is passionate to share with a wider audience. http://www.rachelmcgrath.net.

THE HORSEY SET
By Lisa Romeo

You knew. You knew I was 19. You knew you were 32 and married and the father of two children. You knew I was attracted to you. I wonder if you knew my attraction (which I didn't even understand at the time) was fueled so much by your position (your celebrity almost) in that rarefied air we both breathed, in that world we both pranced through – you with ease, me with longing – that dazzling playground scented with horses and money and blue ribbons, with Hamptons houses and equestrian estates and show horses that cost most than my father's house. Did you know that?

When you flirted with me in the horse show office, when you accidentally brushed against me in the stabling tent, when you waved at me from the rail, when you winked at me from under your hat brim on the sidelines of the polo field, did you know that I thought it was about me? Did you know every time I saw you across a field, across a barn aisle, across the table at a fundraiser, that I wondered if you were there because I was there and not because you were always there? That I didn't understand it was about you and what you could do, get away with, possess, mark?

You knew, I think, that I couldn't enter that world, not completely, on my own, with my marginal riding skills and small trove of not-always blue ribbons and my father's money that seemed so endless on our split level cul-de-sac, but so puny compared to what the horsey daughters of billionaires spent on their third-string jumper.

Did you know you'd get me, from the start? Did you know I would forget myself, lose my compass, imagine there was a good reason for doing the thing I knew I shouldn't be doing? Yes, of course you knew, because that was your game, though I wouldn't know that until you were long gone and I'd meet other young single girls you'd tempted before me, after me.

Did you know that when everyone seemed to know about us, and looked the other way, that I'd think at first that was exciting, edgy, and intoxicating? Of course you knew that; it was part of your charm, as much as your not-so-elegant looks and not-so-refined laugh and not-so-trim physique (though you kept that garbed in preppy pinks and greens, web belts and logo polo shirts).

Here's what I knew: You moved me closer to the pulsing epicenter of that world I knew I'd never penetrate on my own, not with my marginal money and my merely mediocre skills in the saddle. You put a hand on my back and winked at the judges and trainers and suddenly doors opened for me, invitations arrived; at shows, between events, I began to sit in the shaded tents at ringside, where I was served crisp salads by fawning waiters, instead of fetching my own lemonade from the snack stand in the dusty Florida haze.

When you died in that horrible accident, when I got the call, or rather when I go the messages (it took only listening to three of the 12 flashing messages that night – *Hi, call me, I have something to tell you...Hi, you need to call me just as soon as you can...Hi, have you heard anything...* for me to know: someone had died) – that's when I understood. That "we" never happened. That your wife had lost you, not me. That your child who died with you was lost. That your child who survived would be lost forever.

I'd be fine. I'd cry, fly to your funeral, sit in the back, slink away before it was over, fly back to school, ride, graduate, ride, date suitable boys, ride, and forget.

As for that world, the one I ached to be part of, I'd continue to tread its perimeter (my go-to-the-head-of-the-line pass having perished along with you), until something else propelled me to its center again; a particular skill this time, not in the saddle, but at the typewriter, chronicling that world.

Years passed. Decades, before I thought about what you must have also known: that I'd remember you, remember us, remember feeling special. Did you also know I'd understand, eventually, the stupid risk, the selfish impulse?

But I'd also understand it was not all unseemly, not all tawdry. That you were sweet, and kind, and, in your unusual way, honest.

You knew that despite all of that, it was, of course, wrong. Wrong of you to hook me in, wrong to pull me in further, wrong to cheat, wrong to let me help you cheat, wrong of me to help you cheat.

Did you know, too, though that many times since that hideous night when I heard what happened to you, I also wanted to thank you? Did you know that the pep talks stretching into the stolen beach house afternoons, that the touch beneath a table when I felt out of place and intimidated by those wealthy people, that the way you gently thrust me forward when I'd have been content to hide behind you, that as much as they were wrong, they were what I needed?

I think you did know that. I think you cared; that in your own unhealthy, convoluted way, that caring was specific and in some way, sincere. But, wrong.

What you didn't get to hear, ever, because I didn't come to it until long after you died, is me thanking you, me angry at you, me frustrated at not knowing what the hell to what went on between us, me (once I was a wife and the mother of two children) livid at you for involving me in something that meant a wife, a mother (your wife, the mother of your two children) - despite her own claims (which friends who knew her longer and better than I ever did claim she made all the time) that she knew and understood and frankly didn't care all that much about your "extra-curricular activities" - something she might have to fear.

Maybe you knew it all. Maybe you didn't know a thing. Maybe it was all just instinct and happenstance, or convenience and some kind of luck, good and bad.

Years passed, decades, before I knew what I should have, could have, said to you. But who thinks of saying those sort of final, important things when you are 19 and sneaking around (even if it's not so-secretly sneaking around) with someone you are supposed to be polite social friends with, someone whose wife has been nice to you, someone who is 32 and tanned and rich and sexy and vibrant and who you expect to see again next weekend, on the showgrounds, at the bar, under an umbrella somewhere with a book and a bourbon?

Years passed, decades, until you, frozen at 32, became someone far younger than I am now, until I had a child older than 19, until I had something to say, and here, I've said it, and in the end, there's only one thing to say and it is perhaps what I should have, could have said to you then, in the beginning, or the middle, or before the end, and that is goodbye.

****

Lisa Romeo is a writer, freelance editor, and writing teacher. Her nonfiction appears in mainstream and literary venues, including The New York Times, O-The Oprah Magazine; Hippocampus, Under the Gum Tree, Sweet, Barnstorm, Under the Sun, Sport Literate; and in several essay collections and anthologies. Her work was nominated for Best American Essays 2014. Lisa is the creative nonfiction editor of Compose Journal, is part of the founding faculty of the Bay Path University MFA program, and teaches at Montclair State University and at The Writers Circle. She lives in New Jersey with her husband and two sons.

WHERE ARE YOU, O HIGH SCHOOL FRIENDS?
By Anita G. Gorman

I like to go on tours - sometimes in the United States and sometimes across the Atlantic. And each time I think I am going to meet someone from high school. Why do I think that? Because every time I go on a tour there are people from New York City. Even if their name tags say Florida or Arizona, I can spot them, since they have not lost their New York accents, and these people still say "on line" for "in line," a habit I had to break since yokels where I live were correcting me. I got tired of saying, "Everyone in New York City says 'on line'; it's just a regionalism, OK?" Besides, now "online" means being on the Internet, so I might as well say "in line" and avoid further conflict and criticism. I could say that we are standing in a queue, but that would seem a bit too British.

I, unlike these faux Arizona/Florida residents, have lost my city accent. Deliberately. And I now live in a fly-over state, though I really hate that term. So there I am on the first day of our tour to _____ (fill in the blank), sporting a tag with the name of my hokey state, trying to be friendly and outgoing, though it's against my basic nature. "Hi," I say, "is this your first trip with this tour company? Wow, it's your eleventh and you've been around the world three times? Jeepers! Golly! Whoopee!" Then I spot their name tag and/or accent and I say, "So, you must be from New York City!" One time - and I am not making this up - I spotted a New York name tag and said to the woman behind the tag, "So, are you from New York City or from upstate New York?" And she, while squinting at my name tag said with a heavy accent, "I'm from Brooklyn. It's one of the boroughs."

Geez, Louise. She didn't think that anyone from my hokey state had ever heard of Brooklyn. Heck, I was born in Brooklyn, though we lived in Queens. My brother and I had to be born at the Brooklyn hospital where our mother trained to be a nurse, no matter how far away it was and no matter that my brother was born while our mother was still wearing her clothes. I even know where the name Brooklyn came from, and Manhattan, and Queens, and the Bronx (Thank you, Jonas Bronck) and Staten Island, too ("It's lovely going through the zoo"). I learned that in fourth grade - not the song, just the facts - from Mrs. Richter when we studied New York City history. In 1609 Henry Hudson in his ship the Half Moon sailed up the Hudson River, only that wasn't its name at the time. He returned in 1610, but I am not sure why. Maybe he forgot something. In fourth grade we were not told about Henry Hudson's horrible death in what is now Hudson's Bay, way up there in Canada. Best to leave him sailing up the Hudson River in 1610 and looking at the Palisades on the left.

But I digress. I was talking about tours, which Henry Hudson did not experience, to my knowledge. On my tours I do a lot of reminiscing about growing up in New York City, except that I lived in Queens, which does not have quite the cachet of Manhattan. But I get some points, I think, from letting people know that I am not from the hokey state listed on my name tag. That's why I toss out names such as Public School 102, Junior High School 73, and Newtown High School, hoping to impress someone. Anyone.

Sometimes before these trips I think about which of my high-school classmates I might meet again. Sure, you may think that the probability is low that I will meet someone from my past, but I don't think so. I mean, I keep going on these trips, and I keep meeting people from New York, so why would I not someday meet one of the kids (now old) who sat next to me in Biology or Chemistry or Latin or Spanish? I have actually met people who went to my high school, but not from the right year. I really want to meet a classmate so I can show off and demonstrate that the chubby, shy, sullen, and dateless girl I was then now looks younger than her advanced age. I would even settle for a classmate from junior high; they can't be all dead, even though seventh grade was a long time ago.

For example, I would like to see Melissa. That's not her real name. No one was named Melissa back then, but that's what I want to call her. She was in junior high with me and in high school, too. A real busybody, she loved to talk and flirt with the boys and pretend to be friends with the girls. One day Melissa was making plans for her birthday party. I hadn't been invited, but I wasn't really upset about it. Melissa, however, had to 'splain to me why I was not on the guest list. "Anita," she said, "I really wanted to invite you to my birthday party but I had to think of my social standing."

Now it didn't really surprise me that my name was absent from her list, but when I came home I told my mother that my presence at Melissa's party could hurt her social standing. I think I even believed that my attendance at the party could be harmful to the birthday girl. My mother, however, was totally outraged, beside herself, apoplectic, ready to call my homeroom teacher or the principal or the police. I'm surprised she didn't call a press conference. As for me, I understood why I wasn't wanted. After all, I was chubby, shy, plain, and the acne that was to plague me for many years had already started. Heck, if I had been having a birthday party, I'm not sure I would have invited myself. Yes, I want to meet Melissa again.

Then there is John, the boy I had a crush on for three years. I would like to meet him again. I picked him for my crush because he was the only boy in my class who was smart, reasonably good looking, and taller than I was. Also he seemed to be unattached when I first met him. We were in a lot of the same classes, but not Spanish or Latin. In Spanish I had a brief crush on a tall guy with a Hispanic name, but he was really bad at Spanish and I was terrific, in spite of my non-Hispanic heritage. Getting back to John: when teachers sent me on errands I would try to walk down the hall or the staircase just when John was approaching, since I knew his schedule. I longed for a date with John. I longed for a date with just about anybody, but it never happened. Then my friend Barbie arranged for a not-so-blind date with Barbie, her boyfriend - who was a friend of John's — as well as a friend of John and me. I have managed to block all memories of this date. I probably acted tongue-tied and stupid or loud and smart-alecky, or both in alternating moments. And no, her name was not really Barbie; the Barbie doll had not yet been invented.

For three years I retained my illusions that at some point John would show an interest in me. It never happened. The final, crushing blow came with the arrival of two French sisters in our senior year. Ooh-la-la! I could muster a Swedish accent at will, thanks to my immigrant parents, but trying to sound French was beyond me, and, besides, I think John would have known that I was pretending.

So I want to meet John again and show him my cute husband who has been part of my life for years and years. I wonder if John would have an old French woman with him if I met him on a tour.

Now here's the really odd part of my story. I finally did meet a classmate on one of those trips. Let me call her Louise. Thanks! And let me tell you what Louise was like in high school. She was tall, never wore makeup, and was the shyest girl I have ever met. She never talked to anyone. She made me seem like a chatterbox, a stand-up comic, a social butterfly. Compared to Louise, I was a queen, or a princess, popular and respected, with my own coterie of lackeys and followers. I was Miss Congeniality, Miss Smarty-Pants (which I still am, by the way), and Miss Comedian all rolled into one. Compared to me, Louise Hunnicut was Miss Silence, Miss Shyness, and Miss Shrinking Violet all rolled into one.

So there I was, before my tour began, looking at the list of people about to become my best friends for the next week. I saw people from Arizona and Florida (who were probably really from New York City) and then I saw the names of people who still lived in New York City and in my mind I did the equivalent of a shout: "Wow! Could there be another Louise Hunnicut? I'll bet that's my classmate. Won't she be surprised and happy to see me, the salutatorian of our graduating class!"

The tour began, and we all straggled into the orientation where we would learn what to do and what not to do and how to behave and what to expect, just like in high school. I spotted her across the room, my high-school classmate, still tall and without makeup and by herself, so I figured she was still shy. I ran over to her, all smiles, eager to see her again, eager to show her how much I had accomplished, how different I now was, though still a bit the same. "Louise, Louise," I said breathlessly, "remember me?" We went to Newtown High School together; we were in so many of the same classes!"

She suspiciously eyed my name tag with my married name and my hokey state.

I called out my maiden name: "Anita! Anita Malmquist! It's me! So nice to see you again, Louise."

Once again my old classmate eyed me and my name tag, squinting as she apparently racked her brain.

"I don't remember you," she said.

"What?"

"I don't remember you," she repeated.

"I graduated second in our class. I edited the yearbook. I was in a couple of plays. We had lots of classes together."

I was getting desperate. Had I been so nondescript in those days that I was now totally unmemorable? Or had Louise been so shy and withdrawn that she never got to know any of us? Oh please, let it be her problem and not mine.

We stood there eyeing each other. "Sorry," she said. "I don't remember you."

It was my problem.

****

Anita G. Gorman grew up in Queens and now lives in Ohio. She is a retired English professor and currently works as a church organist and choir director. In her spare time she plays the fiddle and guitar with a group of traditional musicians. She has had academic articles published in Mythlore; CLUES: A Journal of Detection; The Swedish-American Historical Quarterly; Dime Novel Roundup; and various reference books, including the Dictionary of Literary Biography. Two of her stories have appeared in Gilbert, the magazine of the American Chesterton Society. Her doctoral dissertation on Jane Austen was published by Peter Lang.

LOVE IN THE PAST AND IN OTHER WORLDS
By Danise Malqui

It was you, as much as I denied it, and said I had moved on. I journeyed off to the southern hemisphere to find oneness with a man of my ancestry, but when I returned, you remained. And when I moved out west, and engaged with the wrong man, my thoughts leapt to you. I've had a few more adventures, but I've returned, and think, now can it be you?

When we first met ten years ago, I was shaken, even before speaking. I knew you little but it was enough to grasp how I thought we were so alike, more than that, like we were each other. How I understood your karma, your causes and conditions, that composed your complexity, your protective introversion, out-of-place nervousness, excessive bossiness. But I knew a tender heart blanketed all of your faults, or absorbing qualities, as I liked to think of them. I palpitated and felt kinship to all of that, assimilated it so easily. My friends would shake their head and say, "nope, not at all" at what I'd say were our similarities. I changed over the years, opened, but I had been like you, and still bear those ancient imprints in my being.

At one point, I asked you out. It was after we had been matched on an online dating website. We had tea and conversation, and afterwards, confusion weighed on me. Whenever we crossed paths, I dodged you. A nervous scared sensitive thing, I was. And then a few months later, we independently, without knowing, rented rooms at the same house. My exhilaration was tempered by shy self-consciousness. We exchanged pleasantries but I shut down when another woman came along. She would moan while doing yoga moves in the middle of the dining room. Daggers would flow through her whenever I appeared or when you paid any attention to me. Eventually, you went with her. And I retreated within, accepting and making new relationships and memories.

I was not in a deep search at that time. I scurried and covered any tenderness, regret, jealousy, anything that budded discomfort.

Then I flowed into new journeys and adventures. I didn't think of you much, perhaps not at all.

But then you came up again. At that point, I was in the middle of deep seeking. It was out west in a spiritual retreat. Our task was to tweeze out the feelings and thoughts of a difficult situation that never felt settled.

In a womb-like yurt, I sat with my two partners and explained that we were housemates and that I liked you, that a woman came along, moaning and stretching, how she would snap at me, how I shut down, how you went with her, how I was silent.

My partners got to work in helping me dig: What did you think? What did you feel? Why didn't you say anything? My hesitations and delicate answers were insufficient for them. They were excavating old bones. And they pushed me along until I discovered what I had felt all that time:

"I didn't think someone could love me. So I didn't try. But I was in love with him."

"That's a really terrible judgment to have about yourself," one partner would say.

And I began laughing, happy to be unlocked. I had a new opening into my heart and mind. I hadn't realized I was in love with you. I couldn't see. I couldn't try back then, and never had tried much at love. I didn't think anyone could love me.

And then, I cried. I cried for the woman I was. I cried in mourning of lost love. I cried for all the people and chances that I let fly away due to fear that nobody would love me.

My tears were an unstoppable stream. My deep inhales and exhales fluctuated with short, cut-off breaths that reestablished the flow in my body. My will to end the tears fought my body's need to release. There was no more hiding.

"Can I do anything to help?" A friend would say.

"No." It was a process I needed to go through – it had been a delayed reaction, a suppression, of multiple years.

I sat in the meditation hall weeping.

And I realized that it wasn't my truth anymore.

By that point, I was in a long journey and in a deep search. I went out west and found my prayers with brothers and sisters of the Red Road, and then I went south to find my ancestral roots. My life was full of fun, new friends and some loves, intermingled with the inevitable hurt and disappointments of any true life lived.

Once I returned and we met up to talk. I discovered that I still love you so easily, in some non-charged simple kind of way. We met one night for dinner. You had ordered appetizers to share with me.

"It's good, what's in it?"

"Chicken."

"I'm vegetarian," I said and spit the food in a napkin.

You felt bad, but I laughed.

I told you about my last year, that I had learned to pray and sing songs. I had wanted to learn songs in case I had a child.

You knew that my question of motherhood had hovered around the last few years. I recounted my story that an elder prayed for me and said: "May this good woman gain clarity if she wants to be a mother of a child or a mother to the world."

You listened with so much wonder and attention and responded, "That's beautiful".

"Do you think I'd be a good mommie?" I asked.

"I think you'd be a great mommie," you responded.

And I was happy.

I left again to pursue romance in Peru, which turned out to be an agonizing education.

And now I know nothing of you. I saw on Facebook that it looks like you're with someone. I'm moderately embarrassed to be writing this, but I don't want to know anything about *it*.

If I could recreate this all, I wonder what would've happened if I had been flirtatious and knew the art of seduction. What would've happened if I had made clear that I wanted to make love to you? But I wanted more than that, I wanted to know you. I wanted to trust you. I wanted that oneness of two beings. I wanted to love you and to be loved.

And what would've happened if "the other woman" hadn't appeared at all? Would there have been someone else? Or would we have formed a simple bond: two friends drifting into lovers? I have no way of knowing if fate had plans of its own and would've turned us both in opposite directions regardless.

Or what if after our first outing, I didn't run away from you but faced you. Would it have been easy then? But then I would've been another woman, with another soul, another karma. I would've been more of the woman I am now.

If I changed the past, I wouldn't be sitting here writing this letter, trying to examine the woman I was, the woman I am and the woman I strive to be.

I've learned some wisdom about this notion of the *past* that we humans cling to. The past isn't static, it moves with us, my teacher once told me. And my ancestral forefathers believed, the past runs here now with the present and the future. The three worlds are here.

So, I can't change the past and our separate fates out of sheer will, fantasy, desire and what if's. I am this woman here flowing through life, interwoven with my past and the unknown. I see that what I do impacts the other worlds.

I hope all of this will help me love, if not you, then myself, and hopefully some other lucky soul.

****

Danise Malqui was born in Paterson, NJ to Peruvian immigrant parents. She holds degrees in History and Urban Planning. It was Danise's dream to explore communal forms of living, Buddhist monastery life and Peru. In 2012, she embarked on a 3-year journey to explore all of that. Danise belonged to the Cusco Writer's Guild in 2015 and began to write creative nonfiction stories about her experiences. Her stories are marked by identity issues as a Peruvian American. She is currently working on her first short story collection entitled "Flowing: a Search for Roots and Grace."

AKA ROBIN
By Cindy Matthews

A window pane rattles in its aluminum frame. There's a damp chill in the bedroom so I tug on a pair of grey sweatpants and a tattered T-shirt. I lean close to a full-length mirror and study my reflection. My neck is smooth except for two vertical, pipe-like wrinkles under my chin; the loose skin jiggles when I shake my head. I decide to head to the living room to see what my husband is up to. The bedroom door sticks when I pull it closed behind me.

Dull morning light streams from the tall windows of our open concept living room-kitchen. The room remains littered with reminders of death. There's a sprinkle of dust on the mantel where an urn once stood, its blond finish identical to our kitchen cupboards. Picture frames hold photographs of our three children and their now deceased grandmother. The loss still swells in the family members left behind and clutches them in its wake. As a show about bank beavers flickers from the TV mounted on the wall, I flip through memories as if they're library index cards.

My husband, John, reclines on the love seat, his right leg gingerly perched on an ottoman. Brand-new crutches straddle the space between him and the door to the deck. When the telephone rings, I'm frozen in place, veiled in sorrow. It is a few days after Christmas. A year and three days since colorectal cancer took my mother.

"Let it go to the answering machine," I say.

John holds the phone to his ear. His green eyes mix with mine. When I detect it might be for me, I groan and wave for him to hang up.

"It's Carl," he mouths, his hand over the receiver. "Cindy's--"

My fingers make slicing motions in front of my neck.

"I know who Carl is," I whisper-shout, working to keep myself under control. Moist hands dangle beside my thighs.

Cindy - my namesake. When I attended elementary school, the only Cindy I knew was a dog. Cindy - the secretary at a school for students with special needs where I work as an assistant administrator.

After he hangs up, John's mouth moves up and down like he's chewing an enormous wad of gum. I only manage to catch a word or two. The words have a quality I don't recognize, the syllables shredding with each motion of his lips. I'm oblivious, as if I'm at the gorilla enclosure at the zoo, the unlatched door to its cage thrashing in the wind. I find myself flushed with fright but of what, I'm not certain. There's a silence that feels too long.

John doesn't have a stake in my fear. He's just broken. Four days earlier he had knee surgery so he's focused on getting off pain medication so he can finally have a Christmas drink. He cradles the phone receiver in his lap as if it's made of egg shell. His lips peel back before he says, "She's nearing the end."

I'd be fibbing if I said I hadn't been expecting this call. I glance out the front window. A young girl clutching ski poles glides past. Her jaw hangs open as she exerts to synchronize arms and legs. My eyes squint against the glare from snow pillowing the front yard. I shudder at the thought of stepping into the frigid air, the roads surely draped in a duvet of snow. Toque and glove weather. Not like when Mother died - a green Christmas - balmy and not a whiff of the white stuff.

"What did you tell Carl?" My fingers fold into each other. "Did you mention the surgery?"

John shakes his head. "I said I'd pass along the message."

I lean against the kitchen counter and pout.

"I had a horrible dream last night," I say. "I was on the roof, refastening the shingles that the wind had ripped off. You were up there with me, trying to stand on your crutches. I kept screaming at you, telling you to get down. But every time I opened my mouth, no sound came out."

John rolls his eyes. "You and your dreams." His eyes are dull. He looks exhausted.

I find myself slamming things--cupboard doors, the lid where the water goes into the coffee maker, the dish washer door--so I pause to take a deep breath.

"In the dream. I woke up before you hit the ground." I feel as though a steel-toed boot is on my chest.

Cindy has end-stage breast cancer. In every bone of her body. I imagine her lying in a hospital bed in their stunningly appointed living room, a stack of pillows cradling her. Physically so frail, it seems the tiniest jostle will split her in two. Her typically fluid movements cut short by the disease. Dark circles around normally sparkly blue eyes. Somehow still beautiful. The floor vibrates with how good she looks despite everything.

Who am I kidding? I can't go and sit there and pretend she has a future. Instead, I hold onto the images from a month ago, when the vagueness of hope remained. Here's the thing. John needs me. What if he fell? I'd blame myself forever and the incident would join a long list of family legends. The loss of life is better kept away, in its place, less able to leave a lasting imprint.

Life makes it a habit to offer signs, indicators of what lies ahead on the horizon.

A few months ago, just before the second diagnosis, Cindy crawled out from behind her work station to show me something. Her insistent gaze reduced me to dust. She gripped a fistful of fat riding along the waistband of her jeans.

"Look at this. If it were a tumor, I'd get someone to cut it off."

"Cindy!" I said, cringing. "How can you say that?"

Her mouth gaped into an O. She had a body that said she'd been able to eat and drink anything she wanted and never knew the cruelty of a diet.

She'd made it to the ten-year mark, cancer-free. Tumors were no laughing matter.

The funeral director who handled my mother's arrangements said eulogies needed to be personal. As I submerge my fingers in tepid dishwater, I consider the attributes of an effective eulogy. What would I share about Cindy? I swish water over a dirty plate and think of the ways in which she is extraordinary. Her voice, distinctive and honest, like syrup in the ear. Her unique smell of lavender and lemons. That gorgeous blond hair, coiffed to perfection, framing her blemish-free face.

But, instead, what pops into my mind is the headscarf she wore the last time we were together, the fabric filled with Monarch butterflies lighting on milkweed, the wings so full of life.

There's comfort in considering the traits that set her apart. The re-purposed whiskey tumbler holding colorful paper clips chained together like train cars. Like how she sometimes called me 'Izzy' and I called her Robin. Pet names reserved for favorites.

Whenever I prepared to leave the school, she'd inspect my teeth for lipstick. The four packets of salad dressing she'd squeeze over a nest of romaine lettuce, making it fit for consumption. Saturday nights playing cards and tipping back a few. How she was the go-to person, everyone's confidante and how little of herself leaked out. Never overly-consumed in the mythologies of her life. I seize these images, putting off the inevitable.

There were things about her that scared me. How she sneaked a cigarette now and again. Those quick flashes of anger at something that upset her at her kids' school. Or the grey pallor that blanketed her when her teen-aged son wrapped his car around a pole. And most recently, that icky green, sweat-grass concoction she choked down in the hopes of delaying her inescapable fate. We exchanged stories like equals, until the disease hollowed out time and drained our daily contact.

John stands on his good leg. He beams at finding the sweet spot on the crutches before crashing back to the love seat.

"Let me help you," I say.

"I can do it myself," he says, the words coming out more sharply than I believe he intends.

I must choose. Decide between them. I'm shocked by the complexity of the decision. I recall the last conversation when Cindy asked me about my 'Freedom 55' plans. Her voice carried less envy than wonder.

There's an awful feeling that fills me, sticky and wet like oriole syrup. Whom would I call to mind John? Everyone we know is away for the holidays. My brain wrestles with what to do. "You ought to go," one side says. "Try and make me," says the other.

I glance out at the front yard where I can barely make out the sidewalk. The snowflakes are tiny with crisp edges. They fling themselves at a peculiar angle from the west. It's settled. I won't drive in a storm.

I've put in my time with the dying. The heavy, drawn-out breaths in the dimly lit room. The smell of copper pennies and the sweat that comes from terror. Fingernails chewed to the quick. Praying for the final inhalation. Only what emerges is a yelp. The looming future reduced to a fizzle, a sorrowful end to an ordinary person's life. Forced closeness so excruciating in its intimacy.

My fingers trace my arm, the skin fresh and prickly with goose bumps, before tears lash my face.

John's voice interrupts. "I'll be okay if you go."

A nervous tic develops near my left eye. Here's the thing. I don't need to go. I know that now. I study the Band-Aid between John's thigh and calf, and sigh. Cindy - AKA Robin - has wrapped a hand around my heart, while mine nestles beside hers. I slide onto the love seat to seek comfort from the rise and fall of John's chest. I lift my head so my lips can brush his cheek.

My voice catches before I say, "I'm not going anywhere."

****

Cindy Matthews has worked as a chambermaid, potato peeler, data entry operator, teacher, and vice-principal of special education programs. She writes, paints, and instructs online courses for teachers in Bruce County, Ontario, Canada. Her fiction and non-fiction have appeared in literary magazines and online in Canada, USA, UK and Australia. "Ringo," a creative non-fiction piece, was awarded third prize at the 2015 NOWW Writing Contest. Her creative non-fiction piece, "Nothing by Mouth," was shortlisted in the 2014 Event Magazine Non-Fiction Contest. Find her work at cindymatthews.ca.

ABOUT THE EDITOR

Former actress and theater director Christina Hamlett is a media relations expert and award-winning author whose credits to date include 31 books, 158 stage plays, 5 optioned feature films, and squillions of articles, interviews and blogs that appear online and in trade publications worldwide. She is also a script consultant (which means she stops a lot of really bad movies from coming to theaters near you) and a professional ghostwriter (which does not mean she talks to dead people). She and her gourmet chef husband reside in Pasadena, California with Lucy, quite possibly the world's cutest Chief Canine Officer.

To learn more about her work, schedule a script consultation, take an online writing class or engage her ghostwriting/editing services, visit http://www.authorhamlett.com

Made in the USA
Charleston, SC
11 November 2015